COLLECTED POEMS

Patricia Dobler

with an introduction by Jean Valentine

Autumn House
Press

PITTSBURGH

Photograph of Patricia Dobler © 2005 by Mark Perrott

Text and cover design: Kathy Boykowycz

Autumn House Press Staff
Executive Director: Michael Simms
Community Outreach Director: Michael Wurster
Minority Outreach Coordinator: Eva Simms
Newsletter Editor: Matthew Hammon
Assistant Editor: Jack Wolford
Editorial Consultant: Ziggy Edwards
Media Consultant: Jan Beatty
Contributing Editor: Susan Hutton

ISBN: 1-932870-05-9
Library of Congress Control Number: 2005900945

Printed in the U.S.A. by Thomson-Shore of Dexter, Michigan

All Autumn House books are printed on acid-free paper and meet the international standards of permanent books intended for purchase by libraries.

The Autumn House Poetry Series

Michael Simms, editor

OneOnOne by Jack Myers
Snow White Horses, Selected Poems 1973-1988 by Ed Ochester
The Leaving, New and Selected Poems by Sue Ellen Thompson
Dirt by Jo McDougall
Fire in the Orchard by Gary Margolis
Just Once, New and Previous Poems by Samuel Hazo
The White Calf Kicks by Deborah Slicer
  (Winner of the 2003 Autumn House Poetry Prize, selected by
  Naomi Shihab Nye)
The Divine Salt by Peter Blair
The Dark Takes Aim by Julie Suk
Satisfied with Havoc by Jo McDougall
Half Lives, Petrarchan Poems by Richard Jackson
Not God After All by Gerald Stern
  with drawings by Sheba Sharrow
Dear Good Naked Morning by Ruth L. Schwartz
    (Winner of the 2004 Autumn House Poetry Prize, selected by Alicia Ostriker)

A Flight to Elsewhere by Samuel Hazo
Collected Poems by Patricia Dobler

Contents

Talking to Strangers

UXB: Poems and Translations

Introduction

I first met Pat Dobler early in September, 2003: Maggie
Anderson came to Pittsburgh to read in the famous Gist Street
series, and she introduced us. That weekend I fell in love with
Pittsburgh, where I was spending the fall semester, and my
visits in those months with Pat, almost always over poetry,
were a big part of that love.

For all their differences, when I think of Pat I sometimes think
of Flannery O'Connor. The tough-mindedness – the passion
– the spiritual life – the humor – and of course, they were
two absolute originals. They were also two who were well
acquainted with illness. And who had an enormous hunger
for life, and for art; and who died too young.

When I think of Pat I also remember James Merrill's descrip-
tion of Elizabeth Bishop, as someone impersonating an
ordinary woman.

Pat's path in her art is one that makes you hold your breath.
As Ed Ochester, one of her teachers, pointed out, in his
introduction to her first book, "It's as though this were not a
first collection but a book by a poet who'd been publishing
for years." You feel in this way that she didn't really start late:
from the start, here was her fierce honesty, and her complete
craft, as well as what Lynn Emanuel has called her under-
stated sophistication.

What grew, of course, was her experience. She moved from
Middletown, Ohio, to Chicago, Iowa, Alaska, Texas, Vermont,
and finally to Pittsburgh where she worked with Louis
Simpson and where her first book, chosen by Maxine Kumin
to be awarded the Brittingham Prize in Poetry, was published
by the University of Wisconsin Press in 1986. She later
traveled to Germany where she translated the work of

Austrian Jewish poet Ilse Aichinger, and finally to Naples in 2002 on a National Endowment for the Humanities Fellowship which inspired many of the poems in her last book, *Now*. The new book is informed by the international world of poetry and translation and history: Milosz, Szymborska, Anne Carson, and Aichinger. She came in her own work to what she described in Aichinger as "the strangeness of the poems [which] belies what seem to be recognizable surfaces." What grew in her was mystery, and her thirst to drink in deeper and deeper histories, and also life "outside of history."

And in *Now*, Pat's work changed further, as Anderson has said, "away from the mortal and the diurnal toward the immortal and the spiritual; some of the last poems seem almost to have been written from the afterlife."

With Aichinger, "a wiser, older woman," Pat had a conversation of mind and heart and language. For over twenty years she was a beloved friend to and collaborator with Anderson, Emanuel and Judith Vollmer. When I first met Pat, though she was younger than me, she seemed to me in some way a wiser, older woman. Although I knew she had been ill, I didn't know how ill she still was; or of course, that soon she would die. I would have asked her many more questions.

Quite close to her death, reading Sappho, Pat had underlined twice:

I think that someone will remember us in another time.

Jean Valentine
March, 2005

Acknowledgments

for *Now*

I wish to thank the Corporation of Yaddo, the National
Endowment for the Arts, and the Pennsylvania Council on
the Arts for their generous support during the completion of
this book.

Heartfelt thanks to Charlotte Mandel, whose sensitive
editorial suggestions and generosity of spirit helped make
this book possible.

—P. B.

for *Collected Poems*

Autumn House Press wishes to acknowledge some of the
people and institutions that made this publication possible:
Sister Grace Ann Geibel, President of Carlow University, for
making grant money available; Samuel Hazo who once again
supported an Autumn House project with vision and tireless
energy; Gerald Stern, Jan Beatty, Ed Ochester, Judith Vollmer,
Lynn Emanuel, and Maggie Anderson, who supported the
project; and Jack Wolford, Matt Hamman, and Ziggy
Edwards who typed and copyedited the poems. We are also

grateful to Ron Wallace and Margaret Walsh of the University
of Wisconsin Press and Peter Oresick of Mill Hunk Books for
generously giving us permission to reprint these poems.
Finally, and most significantly, we recognize the generosity of
Stephanie Cerra and Lisa Mullen, Pat's daughters, for giving
permission to publish all of the poems Patricia Dobler wished
to see in print.

Dobler, Patricia. *Talking To Strangers*. © 1986. Winner of The
Brittingham Prize in Poetry. Reprinted by permission of The
University of Wisconsin Press.

Dobler, Patricia. *UXB*. © 1991. Reprinted by permission of Mill
Hunk Press.

All other poems in this collection: © 2005 by the estate of
Patricia Dobler.

Every effort has been made by Autumn House Press to acknowl-
edge the previous publications of poems which appear in this
collection. If any previous publication of these poems has not
been acknowledged, please contact the publisher, and correc-
tions will be made in subsequent editions.

NOW

2005

This body so fragile and woundable,
Which will remain when words abandon us.

Czeslaw Milosz, *"Body"*

for Stephanie Cerra

I

January

More snow, the weather's raw,
as if something certain
circles near but hides
won't make itself clear.

The larger flakes fall upward,
the sycamore's slim branch
yields to snow.

The brief shining of my mother
in this world. How is it with her now.
It's the wolf moon, mother,
and his indifferent eye.

The Gift

Walking next to the Clarion's clear water,
I kept pace with a doe on the other bank
or encountered three different animals

aware of me and warily cropping the same
grasses, wearing the same dun color
while I struggled with the day, the light,

the blue sky like a hammer, fighting
an idea, that the past can return (long terrible
days howling what no one can translate)

letting this idea become a gift and the brilliant
day an eyesore. She or they munched
while a semi flew like a bullet from Ohio to Pittsburgh.

One of them, if there was more than one, twitched
her flanks and rose with the gnats behind the swallowing green.

Ars Poetica

She said: When leaves turn yellow in the high mountains,
we sit in the woods for the elk. You go where they are and sit.
You don't chase them or kill them when they are in rut, you
don't hunt them at all or you risk spoiling the meat. And you
shoot once, into the body. Bear hunting is different, since
you're not after the meat. But you must not *think* Bear. Or
Bear will know and you will become the hunted.

Prayer

Uncle Jim brought her the first tomato
from his garden; she wouldn't share it.
We were happy, she wanted something.

We emptied her bureaus
knowing she didn't want her things
put out for sale, fingered by anyone.

We wept when we saw the small suitcase
she pulled everywhere,
the yellow yarn bow on its handle.

Today I found her bible. An emery board
fell out of it, like the relic of a saint.
How like my mother

to give herself a manicure
and spiritual improvement at once.
Let me see her, let me see her again.

Last Cigarette

She bums a cigarette from the wrecker driver,
looks out at Alaska with its 15 kinds of snow in June,
the wizened foot-high hundred-year-old pines.

She hates this place, is glad they're driving home
which is why she drove the jeep into a ditch
flying over the slither of mud highway

So hellbent to get back she could have killed
them all, her little girls, her husband.
Her lover's back home. She sucks it in.

Her Plan

If she could call, the past
might suddenly come back
and there she'd be with only

foreign money in her purse...
She wants to die
no more than necessary.
What if she took leave

of her senses and went back
to the nothing-well one last time?
There is, and for everyone,
a final room to enter,

a single room to which
each of us is drawn.
The poet she loves best has said,
"Great misfortune simplifies."

The next poem tells you how to live.

Scarification

She has lived through the simplifying
of a great misfortune.
She thinks about changing her skin
from the outside in.
She tries to think about words
as jars that have come through the fire.
Considers
the scarification of adolescents
and the tattoo meant to protect
from disaster,
the tattoo on the lips
of Maori women to show they are married,
the belief in the hearts of Ainu women that
without the tattoo
the devil with blazing sword will scar them
after they die. Better the scars she chooses;
tougher than skin, they might be jewels, scarab,
carapace on flesh.

The Heroine

Red smudge of moon; a thumbprint.
She was under the thumb, engaged
(along with the fog which entered
as if it knew the weight
of implication) in a self-wounding
narrative – her role was that
of a tourist in her life; she also played
a bewildered animal who stepped
into the clearing, trailing two cubs
and a man who wished to document the scene.
She called it a life but it seemed to belong
to someone else; she was always waiting
for some business to be over so the real play
could begin. She remembered being bound
to a great enterprise that called
for a rapture, an ecstasy of sacrifice,
her massive strength exerted on behalf...
(here the plot grew foggier)...
                    What rose
unbidden from her was a kind of trance, an enmeshing
under the bruised and sullen moon, a rage
so intoxicating it sent the man and the little ones
to sleep, so that she stood alone there, she and the moon.

The Fashion of Divorce

In her new fashion, she developed habits: got up, made bed, fed cat, cleaned litter box, fetched newspaper, made coffee, poured juice, toasted bagel, waffle, bread. (This fashion varied.)

She could set her clock by her.

Went to work, returned before dark in summer, after dark in winter, cooked dinner, poured wine, read book, slept. On the left side of the bed.

The Secret

The woman who carries a secret has exhausted herself with its weight. She delivers it into the pocket of her dream in which she has become an officer, alone on horseback. He has not abandoned his men, but has sought a moment outside the enterprise of war that focuses and consumes him. Like the woman, he is exhausted. The morning drizzle soaks his long gray cape. His horse is well-lathered; the officer has ridden hard this morning and his thighs still tremble, the saddle creaks beneath him as he shifts his weight. A calm moment; the epoch indeterminate. He holds a twist of paper into which he puts ripe cherries, for he has paused along a road lined with cherry trees, and in the gloom the fruit seethes with color and its own round nature. Surcease of sorrow. He eats the cherries one by one. Then he is riding wildly toward a burning village, he knows that sweet sick odor. With a howl, the woman possessed of a secret opens her eyes. He prods his horse straight into flame.

Contention

Body my dear, my runaway,
don't leave me forever,
Body my own.

But come back without
your costume of aches and no breath,
the scant teaspoons of sleep

you gave me, and those composed
of bristles and points.
And the mental weather!

You had me storing scarves
in the freezer, trying
to punch holes with a broom

in the ceiling for air.
We have been friends,
but now you are engaged

in this over-the-top
disgraceful performance. Still,
eat a little something.

Let us reason together, forgive
and I will pardon you,
old buddy. My old pal.

Post Office Clock

The clock in the post office counting down,
so many seconds left in the 20th century,
and there you are holding your package,
a gift for a child, a book about corn
and Indians, and time is slipping by
second by second; it is of course always
slipping by, but you are not always so brutally
reminded of it; the bright red numbers
blinking off into the void; it is appalling
that every human being has to croak and
no exceptions to the rule, no improvisations.

Such an outcry about the clocks that
the U.S. Postal Service threw them out.
Good. Nothing is stopped but
imagine that beautiful child always
happy with his new book, always new.

In the Pain Clinic

All of us are whining.
No one wants to be here.
We all like and also hate
the healthy one the therapist

who tells us to breathe deep
to visualize to share.

No one wants to be here. We all hate
the one twisted with arthritis
the whiplash the chronic fatigue
the skinny one who can't breathe.

This is America! We are Americans!
This is the fate
we are intended to escape.
No one wants this country open to death.

We want the healing of the wound
not the wound that can't be closed
not this loosening in the dark.

Outside the civilians
lick their ice creams with pink tongues.
Somewhere fireworks are prepared
ephemeral and booming.

Her Return

Sappho turns herself over
as if she herself is a garden
to dig into and turn, turn again.
    Glistening and restless,

she is what lifts to the light
after the great fire has left
a world half-consumed so that
    outlines of garden

benches, what had been trees,
seem real until she breathes on them.
They shudder and collapse,
    ashes to ashes.

Among the ruins and the bones
she will be heard, torn, interrupted
and brief, about letting
    go without breaking.

Foreign Dream

I don't seem to have even a bit part
in my dreams anymore,
my dreams are mob scenes,
a huge house-party at a stately home,
ok, wait a minute, more like the houses
where I baby-sat as a kid, or an immense
cocktail party in my old college dorm but with men.
Or it's a restaurant-bar somewhere in wartime Germany;
all at the great long table are frightened. It's dark,
a black-and-white film, I can flit in the dark
from face to face. Everyone smokes.
One woman, handsome but no longer young,
says of an absent friend, "She is dangerous."
All the white still faces at the table agree
with this assessment. And suddenly I'm inside
one of these people. I don't know who.
Someone at this table is a version of me.

II

Angel

The nurse was big and black and really pissed at the little girl, the only kid on the burn ward. "Your daddy's out there crying and here you lie in the dark, shame on you, young lady, you *best* start eating and drinking!" The nurse screeched the blinds up and glared.

The girl didn't care, just wanted her way, to be dead. She thought refusing to live was better than using poison or a knife or gun. An 11-year-old Jesuit. But the big nurse had guilt as the girl's number and scared her good. Or maybe she dreamed up the nurse.

Zonked on morphine most of the time, she read anything to escape her body: tales of singers who traveled in pairs and sang angelic love for their Lady, who believed the body was a prison for the soul or just a veil, a shift of dust motes that colored the air.

She learned to step out of her body, observed from above the people in white who had to deal with her face, her arm in its putrid bandage. She learned to believe in accidents, that she was caught by fire, not unlike those troubadours who caught their feet in the Church's webs.

As for the nurse, a dream or not, she was a messenger from the real world who trusted in the narrow transom of the will: water down the throat, pudding from the cold spoon, fruity ices to be sucked on, oh black angel who made the girl live.

Burned Away

Margaret is more beautiful now, thinned out.
She sits at ease, calm, smiling
like an icon. Her husband serves her
as years before she served him.
He pins the curlers in her hair,
dresses her, sits her on the toilet.
The other women in the home cry, heartbroken.
"I'm a good girl," one of them says.
But all of Margaret's passions are
burned away, those years of slaving and scrimping
gone, forgotten, her mind is simply consumed.
This summer his grapes are thickening, ripening,
better than they've been in years,
and now he cannot tend them.

Poem

Even now the memory surprises:
his clear blue eyes suffused with panic –
but he was never afraid, his confusion lifted
for a moment when he saw death looking at him,
what came would come,
he would face it as he always faced the unknown,
with anger and contempt; nevertheless
she saw his fear as he met the void.

That Time

I didn't like men
Didn't like women
Children bored me

Long snows collapsed
outside the kitchen door
freezing it shut

I forced the vacuum's
beater bar into
the dirty plush

As for sex   that burden
that charm of betrayal
that got me there in the first place

I chilled
Laid up walls of books
I was besieged and fell asleep

The elaborate dinner parties
of the 60's
My thick greased cookbooks

Julia Childs' fluty Boston voice
The trips to three libraries
Bags of novels consumed

The idea was
to float and get numb
Yet the children were so beautiful

Their sweet weight hung about me
Still it was weight
The fruits of my choice

I lacked cleverness   lacked wit
Would have chewed off my foot
if that could've answered it

Choir

All the morning light has gathered
on this street in a glimmering tunnel.
Donna hates her mother, tells her so,
tells the street and all the windows,
but it's early, eyes are mostly shuttered,
a very few old women of this street
stroll away from the church at the end
of the lit tunnel. They assemble
in front of Donna's house, argue
in harsh Italian. Then a thin
treble, a single voice that
sharpens itself on the morning,
insists on a minor, a gaunt and tart,
a vinegary melody, black
as their dresses. When they finally
laugh together, that sound takes ragged flight
to the window of someone who's watching.

Unheimlich

Always out late, the old couple walk
what must be their child,
a merest bundle of sticks,
all angles and lurching gait, but there's
no telling how old he is. He makes odd –
one couldn't call them "calls" – utterances,
not really "distress cries." Years ago
the woman would walk him around
their front lawn, her hand over his mouth
to muzzle him, for his noises
do disturb – they are so close to sounding
human. But none of this seems *unheimlich*,
that is, "uncanny." Eventually
they will loosen their hold on him, of course,
that's to be expected. But no,
what seems strange in the hot night
is this very late tolling of a single chime
or bell, an ice cream truck calling
to the nearly deserted street.

Backroads

The night was sweet with cut grass and the smell
of sticky macadam and they were sweet dumb seventeen

driving next to ripening cornfields on Ohio two-lanes
summer nights in the 1957 red caddie rag-top

45-rpm record player where the glove box should have been
his disconcerting lizard way of licking his upper lip

nearly to the tip of his squashed boxer nose the first person to play
the Brandenburg Concertos for her and how 19th C. and
    pre-sexual

this sounds but sex was only part of the mysterious wild hunger
that propelled them out into the cornfields looking for cows to tip

not the compote of fruit glowing in the cut glass bowl each
    Sunday
that they were supposed to want but their animal longing

for the still warm point about which the universe wheeled
it exploding for them like honeysuckle when you bite

into the little buds and your mouth fills with gold.

The Joke

At her prize summer job in Sorg's paper mill she tested
Samples of vellum carried messages to the mill floor typed

The occasional letter fetched mail and coffee a plum job
As she was reminded rather often as she was reminded

She was smart and lucky with her scholarship her 17 years
Her long legs that got her noticed by the married guy

In the lab but she liked when they let her work in the lab
Its air-conditioning its windows overlooking the Great Miami
 River

Hardly a river more a slow-moving mass of pea-colored sludge
That no one remarked on including her because even she knew

If you wanted a paper mill and its jobs you had to take green
 muck
For a river and after all what did it matter she would not be here

Come fall (it could not come fast enough she *was* blessed) and
 the smell
From the factory floor the wet smell of gluey cardboard coming
 apart

The rolls of waste paper taller than the marble columns of
 Cincinnati's
Railroad station from which she would depart (never to come
 back)

Had nothing to do with her and her will what she wanted oh
her hidden
Rituals to bring luck and solitude and silence to the clang of the
mill

And she will need to please no one but herself not smile
when there's
Nothing to smile about not pretend to be a good girl a hard
worker

And blind to the pitiful pursuit of the guy in the lab his stupid
going-away
Present: a large bottle of sulfur-colored liquid meant to be
a joke.

Jazz

Chicago how I loved you
my release my out of jail my joy
the sweet heat of the drinks in those clubs
under the city, southern comfort on the rocks
always late at night smoky horns
underground underneath the city streets and rain
falling from far away, another world, always dripping
down there from the arms of the El around midnight.

I was so blonde I stuck out like a flare
so tall I had to bend just to get down there
where the music was succulent like honey
oh it was before the 60's I could go to those clubs
sticking out like I did because I loved that jazz
and it didn't matter how corn-fed
and blank I was, I felt the sweetness,
I was indulged even in my whiteness,
even I could hear the intricate unwinding
of the riffs careening from the alto sax.
I knew nothing at all, not what the music
cost, nor what would break loose or how soon.

Eschatology

Where the clock carried its worst hour
where the circle lived inside the wedding ring
where they erased the story until it became water
sliding over stone
where the earth answered the glacier
showing on its body innumerable paths;
that is, there in the place
that felt like an eye gouged out,
a local place, a habitation
with its household *numen*, god of the slag-heap,
the place a house in which she lived
and where she studied the last four things:

what connected the time assigned to her
with the time of everyone else?
what bound the man and woman?
for whom was the table set?
what did they learn
as the thread played out?

– Silence, the emblem
between the damaged
and the damaged,
between them,
no secrets.

There was a door.
It had a handle.
The wheel rolled out of itself,
printing on the floor
unanswered questions.
What held her there
sheeted with ice
like a good tool left outside?
Where were the letters she delivered,
knowing they were lies?
What waited for those
who lived in their lives like renters?

– The separate rooms,
wherever they might be, farther away
from anywhere than anything else in the world.

Insight

The left eye can read books,
the right one interprets highway signs.
They have learned to work apart,
one near one far.
They accommodate each other,
and though the world
they report on is flat,
you have come to accept their evidence.

Now that we know one of us
will not see the other one
out of this life,
we are learning to accommodate
the collusion of us both
in the general calamity.

On the one hand
a basket of glitter,
some days like single jewels,
and on the other
a hard and singular certainty:
one of us will not see
the other out.

Now

The world is inviting this August night and I can fly
Anywhere but choose to stroll under familiar lampposts

Near houses shuttered with only a few dim lights
Showing two orange cats who watch me suspiciously even
    though

I feed them their kibble but they have trouble recognizing me
A half-dressed ghost floating light-headed above the loose stones

And cobbles like the back streets in Budapest where people are
    familiar
With the notion that history begins with war and that this
    fleeting grace

This present that is now the past is like revisiting one's child
    hood home
Which can't be taken on its own terms because places and people

Have nothing to say to us now whereas they used to mean
    everything
And we have lost something the naming of which escapes like
    mist

And the vague importance of this loss makes the bright and
    shallow
Immediacy of now taste of popcorn not a meal with wine and
    friends

Not anything as real as the perfect moon head of the baby who
    rises
Over his father's shoulder and grins because he's dressed for
    vespers

In a sailor suit with bare feet and I have to wonder where is the
    essential
Balefulness of human nature in which I am a true believer
    where is that

Predatory eat up everything on the ground before us our locust
    nature now
But I myself love my predator cat her stalking leap on my
    ankles her yellow eyes

The long black muscle of her body how she holds my arm
    down pins back
Her ears and bites and I delight in the nowness in which I
    cannot trust.

An Afterlife

I climbed to the third floor,
I climbed and could still breathe
the thin bright air.
Last year I thought I never would again
climb and breathe.

The attic door opened a crack
to a table set for one,
a silver spoon and fork,
a vase with white roses, bowls filled with food,
all of it smelling delicious: borscht
sprinkled with dill, salmon in a kind of sauce,
a bright red vegetable

I couldn't name, for I was on a porch
somewhere in Russia somewhere in the country,
long shadows fell on the white table,
I thought it must be a white night,
the vines were heavy, the porch's lattice-work
was carved with rooster, horse, man.

The one chair, pulled away
from the table, was ready to hold me.

Decree

Here in Greece it is late,
very late here in Rome,
late all over the empire
of your century, and here
especially it is easy
to sleep and stay asleep.
Those slow walkers whose eyes
follow you in your dreams –
you will pass them,
once you are awake, with eyes
averted. The fat young woman with no claim
on you, neither daughter nor friend,
her plastic sandals, her bluish feet
dangling over the edge, don't look too closely
into the pale eyes she rubs
like a tired child. Accept
you are one of us, the blessed
of these latter days.
And how dark the short days!
But for now you must sleep.
Go to sleep; stay there.

III

On the Way to a Meeting

In January my boss asked me
if I had seen the full moon
the night before, the hunger moon,
the wolf moon, we were headed
toward a grievance committee.
I lied and said yes because
suddenly I could see that other moon
hanging as if by a thread
over the Bay of Naples.
The whole improbable golden orb
of it, laying a path we could walk on,
how could we not think of love songs
with rhymes on the ooo sounds,
with that pregnant opulence
glistering away! But here I was
having just lied to my boss,

because I had lost track
of the moon's phases,
hadn't looked out the window in months.
Back in June back in Naples
the slight rain intensified
hibiscus, roses, the various herbs,
there were no windows, just hairpin turns
and bougainvillea, I had lost track,
I didn't know or do I lie,
I didn't want to know how sick she was,
she was dying while I was moon gazing,
the wolf moon was already eating her
and I stood with my friends drinking wine.
If she had known what I was doing
she would have been happy for me,
my mother, her one talent was loving.
Mine is grieving.

Home-Brew

Betty's age was a secret   She lied to the foreman   She
was only 17 but lucky enough to look older and her sister Mary

backed her up   Mary was a good fast tobacco can packer
so when the foreman found out he didn't get mad

just put Betty on piecework so she worked 8 hours a day
Short time   Betty was quick like her sister   They soon

worked the night shift together   It was 1930   They had to sneak
out a side door after work avoiding their girlfriends from school

who asked can you get me on at the factory?   This from girls
who had finished high school   Sex was a secret from everyone despite

the hillbilly girls who talked all night about things Betty didn't
   understand
Men and what they did with women   She felt nervous enough

at the rolling tables where she hoped she did a good job packing
the cans of Union Leader so when the girls teased her she was glad

that between the clank of the line and their hillbilly talk she barely
   understood
a thing   The job was ok   She had her sister to walk home with after
   their shift

but when they hit the old school-yard the trees' deep shadows
   spooked them
and they ran the last mile home   Were those man-shapes under
   the trees

Still they kept their fears to themselves and knew their luck to
   be working
while the steel and paper mills moldered To be young but to
   look old

and while they ran they could smell their mother's home-brew
   Another secret
the whole neighborhood knew and kept because Mom made
   good home-brew

They drank it chilled   it tasted bittersweet

On the Lie

It has broken us crushed us drowned us
The wind has consumed us swallowed us
As timber is devoured by fire from heaven

"The lie stuck in his throat" can this happen
I can only report on what was said
Knives gossip among themselves

In the kitchen drawer they are planning
It has broken us crushed us drowned us
What sticks in the throat in the throat

The ivory flenser cool curved and slender
Separates the harp seal from its fur
I can only report on what was said

The wind has consumed us swallowed us
Look on us with pity we who only report
It has broken us crushed us drowned us

Voices reach up like arms to rap on shutters
As timber is devoured by fire from heaven
The lie that reports on what was said

Sticks in the throat the untruth that which is not
Of the star-bright kingdom of heaven can this
Happen as timber is devoured by fire from heaven

Persephone's Blues

Well, thought I was in mother's house
And sleeping in her bed
Dreamed I was in mother's house
Asleep in her soft bed
Then I woke up and knew that she was dead

I know I'll never find her
In the tatters of this world
She's gone and I can't find her
O the fabric of the world
Is torn; she never said a word

Let the corn and fruit be blasted
Let the rivers wipe their eyes
O corn and fruit, be blasted
You rivers, wipe your eyes
My mother's gone and left me
And I can't be satisfied

Body Secret

Before they learned to render the body
the artists mastered draperies. So they covered
the Aphrodite with quiet face and crimped hair
from neck to little foot. Her toes
peek out and she extends a hand, the same pose
you see in countless later Mary statues.

This hidden body suggests a severe goddess
yet there were those who loved her – thousands
of offerings from centuries of supplicants
were found: terra cotta replicas of pomegranates,
babies in swaddling bands, sometimes
wombs or doves or sheaves of wheat.

They're powerful, these mothers of the gods,
but my mother loved the lesser saints
with their minor tasks: Anthony the finder,
Joseph the husband. When she was dying
and couldn't pray any more and was angry,
I didn't talk to God or Mary, I wanted her husband,

my dead father. "Daddy," I said. "You have
always loved this woman, now look at her.
Tell God." I have no votive offering, and for sure
Daddy was not one of the great ones, but he heard me.
In the morning I went to her bed and found
the still body, the little foot stuck out of the sheet.

Mother and the Diver

The diver at Paestum, the slim body
entering a mirror of blue water,
poised, serene, while his friends
eat & flirt & philosophize...
The painting shows a happy death,
a cheery departure, this plunge of the soul
into the unknown, the soul that leaves
and still remains... lovely to think so,
to paint it so on the fine walls of his tomb.

I want to believe in this. The diver
wears only his archaic smile.
Balance, order, and proportion
rule. Death is put in his place... I want
to believe this but I know she will never
come back to me. How is it that the diver
inclines to his pool, the boys & men
drink wine, touch each other, each lives
in his own way & I am still wracked

and torn. When she lay dying her brothers
& sisters gathered to tell stories, they laughed
so hard Lisa worried & said Grandma
does all this noise bother you? Honey
said my mother, they're celebrating my life.
Maybe that's why, while Lisa nursed her new
son, she felt Mother's strength
like a breeze, a cool hand on her cheek.
She believes this. It's lovely to think so.

Fortification

In the car, in the cemetery for the famous,
I have found a good place to wail –
people will think I'm another mourner.
Brown seed-balls hang by the hair
from the sycamores. Late afternoon light
should be swallowed by now, but there's
a glow from someplace, probably the snow itself –
let it be gone. And it's far too late
for that lineman to see what he's doing,
shinnying up a tree with his ropes and electric saw.
But those branches have to go.
Let me be practical and clear:
I am not this sycamore, nor is it a figure for me.
Someone I loved is not dead but gone.
When the lineman lops off the offending arms,
I can see the tree's pale under-skin below
its greenish bark. Not a dark tree. An embattled one.

Tonino's Fingernail

His double life, who wouldn't love it, you could be responsible,
a family man eating your Sunday pasta, but you could
still be operatic like the men at the funerals Tonino shows us –
the great masses of flowers the blunt-nosed hearses
the abstracted men in silk suits and all of them dangerous,
what will they do next? For that matter
what will Tonino do next with his little fingernail,
manicured, long and curved? Then Ignazio
and I lean over the wall of a villa, Vesuvius in the distance –
he's a jumped-up scion of English shopkeepers,
lives here like a king – he tells me Naples is beautiful
but watch the inhabitants, their cunning is unbearable. But
I like the city with its pickpockets at Mass and weird aquarium
(no colorful tropical fish, just the kind I'll see on tonight's
      dinner plate)
the dusty parks and teen-aged brides arranged on harbor rocks:
one throws her head back and lets her sleeves fly free –
then she's embraced by her balding groom and arranged,
      arranged
again by bustling men who fuss over her, snapping pictures,
a baby-toting woman stands watching. It's life, friends.
All the 20th century's best ideas ended in disaster
but that's irrelevant in Naples. Are there babies? And
how's business? Mille, mille, mille, says Tonino.
He's talking about time, thousands of layers of occupiers,
and the cynical ancient poor, how do they go on
and over and under your life, doubling, tripling.

Rich and Poor

As the rich become supremely rich
they disappear
invisible in their silences
they could be doing anything
behind their great walls.

Sometimes they are too visible –
great land masses pushing around the globe,
inventing Australia. Meanwhile the poor
rise like islands, lifting their profiles
to passing ships but keeping their green secrets,
their litter and wood-smoke, at the ends

of their own bad roads. And the rich,
who do not long to be understood,
who can't get to those green secrets
and are indifferent to them, need
only to be untouchable.
In this, they resemble the poor.

Who do you dislike the most, the rich or the poor?
Consider poor Robert in Cannes, recovering
from his eye-lift operation, who couldn't see
any of the flowers of Grasse, and who sympathized?

Not I.

The Day After

So I walked back to the place we'd found him,
needing to see the blood stains and my hands
in the place his head had lain.
He had been a bundle by the road edge,
a black man lying face down, his blood running down the hill.
You had a flashlight, played it over the body,
said his head was stoved in, you saw the brain tissue.
I tried to run away. What if the attacker
was still in the park? What if
he could see us? Therefore what were we doing?
You stood by the body,
flagged down a car, ordered
cops and ambulance while I listened
to the man's heavy liquidy breathing.

Next day, I understood that he had been
a human still alive when the others joined us
and authority took over.
The man died, the murderer confessed,
no mystery there, they had been friends,
sang in the same church choir, the killer
hung himself in his cell.
No one can tell this story.
All of us are held outside
on the knife-edge.

History

Hamlet needed to set things right
but he lacked a certain ruthlessness.
My mother had it, in spades.
When she closed a door, it stayed closed.
I tend, like Hamlet, to leave it open a crack.
In Germany – a minute, reader,
before I get back to Elsinore and Mother –
there was a little walk through a manicured wood
most quickly got to by a shortcut through
a simple meadow. And in that meadow,

by whatever quirk or accident of air, earth,
altitude, depression – a kind of fog.
Not deep, the bowl of that meadow, but chill,
and, because it was Germany, fraught. Because
weeded-over railroad tracks wandered through
there was also tragic darkness: memory's
boarded-up house, smoky warren of the past
never sorted through, the mess of history,
but, most peculiar, an atmospheric change
just there, a few feet in every direction,
a drop in temperature,
a frisson, a lurch in the belly,
someplace strange.

The dead should stay dead,
we don't like it when they come visiting
with their to-do lists. All that unfinished
business, all those scores they mean to settle.
Go home, ghosts, we want to say,
but then there'd be no play, no history.

Mother broke an engagement to an otherwise
suitable and handsome young man
because he once came onto his mill shift drunk,
nearly killed a man. Grandpa saw,
chewed out Mother about it and bam,
the guy was history. She never regretted it,
not for a minute, but I am full of second thoughts.
The war has been over for decades,
my parents dead for years, my own marriage is dead,
and still I go back
over the ground to pick at what I can.

Here and Now

Maybe it is self-hatred when a girl
offers the nipple and labia to be pierced
or gives over her canvas of waist and thigh
to the inked needle; but the little kingdom of the body
is all that she commands. For certain there is rage
about death, and here and now, the anger
of any boy on the street, that blond boy striding
on the far edge of the sidewalk who takes a decision
not to yield an inch to the woman
not looking, who swerves into him,
to whom he mutters "asshole," his greased hair picked out
in a halo of anger, his face an eruption
turned against, how could it matter, any one
of the tourists on this pretty street in this pretty town.

An artist went dancing with the locals, offered his hand
to a guy who ground out a cigarette in his palm –
it's edgy here, elaborate floral "arrangements"
on the traffic islands, a heap of blanket,
paper and human in the park, bespoken rehabbed B&B's,
the town's fully occupied, some drunken
half-dressed boys and girls get carted off by the cops,
the children slit a lip or nostril of their kingdoms.

Corpus Christi

Last year, watching the games on TV, the perfect Olympiad
  bodies –
leaping spinning running – they had nothing to do with me.
Envy was beside the point. I did not recognize them.

In the hospital my roommate was a hundred year old woman.
A little husk of a woman.
She cried for water, water, water.

I'm HONGRY, I'm HONGRY, she said.
Her, I recognized.

•

And abandoned wasps' nest, each of the five-sided papery holes
perfect but empty, hollowed out. That was my body.

The faint apparitional days
punctuated only by smells.

I craved coke ovens. Cheap Wal-Mart clothes, oil soap,
whatever was pungent or clean.

A visitor stood forever in the afterimage of his scent.
It hung, hung on the air. More real than he was real.

What could be seen trembled from sight. What could be heard
faded, not like a train rushing past, more like a dress fades

from red to pink to white, like frowzy heads of fallen peonies.

●

The old woman when she was well
took care of an even older brother.
She was there for a rest, but the family needed her home.
From 2 until 4 in the morning: I'm HONGRY, I'm HONGRY.

●

The feast was Corpus Christi, relentless.
The monstrance a sunburst
in the priest's two hands, high above us all.

In the center that which must be seen.
My flesh is true food, my blood true drink.

That which cannot be avoided.

Inexorable. Eat this body, drink this blood.
This is a hard saying, said his disciples.

And the woman, a shadow with teeth, a will with a mouth.
As for me, I could not breathe and eat. I had to choose.

It was as if someone had asked me a question, how much
do you love your body?   And I had to answer, not that much.

Because I had to choose, I chose to breathe not eat
and therefore chose the rack of my shoulders,
the teeth huge in my face, the pelvis a complicated cup.

•

The frazzled nurses were glad to see the back of her.
Released, silent and ramrod-straight in the wheelchair,

she looked at me once. One slow turn of head. Her ancient
turtle eyes passed over me, and she moved into a future.

What rearrangements her fates were forced to make.
I recognized her: implacable, eating, drinking.

Say This

Say she works in a steak-house but has bigger plans.
Say she's got one kid and one in the oven.
Say she's 17,
and when she ran away from home
she told her mother, "I want to have Justin's baby,
don't try to stop me."

The family agrees
she's a smart girl, could have been
an engineer, a lawyer, and here's what
she's chosen: the trailer, the waitressing, her soap operas,
the talk show opinions and "something of her own" –
two babies from two fathers. She wants
this because she wants this.
Her life keeps snapping at her ankles,
backing her into a corner,
and she doesn't seem to notice.

The family mulls it over.
The oldest sums it up: "I'll say this
for her... she's not afraid of work."

Say this while she lifts her trays
of steaks and margarined potatoes, say this
as she makes her 7 bucks an hour, say this if she takes
the kid's fathers to court or takes them to bed
(she works hard she's not afraid of work) and argues
with her mom about those bigger plans that are no secret, not
    secret at all.

_____ IV

Train Bike Flivver Droshky

1

Many bullet-shaped train cars
steel turquoise silent slow –
I'm driving alongside them
as they roll toward me,
my little flivver's
top is down, I'm reasonably happy.
Then I'm driving on the tracks
& the turquoise train cars are headed
straight for me so I abandon
the tracks for an open field.

2

Dorothy Hosner trekked
through middle Europe in the 30's
alone on a bike. She wrote
"Cycling Across Roumania" and
"Pedaling Through Poland,"
breathless accounts
w/ her own pix
for *The National Geographic*.

3

This was one hell of a magazine. That yellow cover, the
globes, the laurel leaves, man's (whiteanglosaxonmaleman's)
observations of remarkable phenomena – volcanic eruptions
undersea bermuda life expeditions to the north pole giant
sequoia trees definitive dates of new mexican ruins scientific
balloons taking a ton of scientific instruments aloft african
maiden's breasts.

4

This dream flivver I'm driving is
a cute little thing, all leather seats
& open. Those turquoise train cars
jump the tracks & aim themselves at me
they roll too slow & can't catch me.

5

Was it John Oliver LaGorce
or Maynard Owen Williams
or some other *NG* editor –
triple-named-wonder
who objected so strenuously
to a lone girl roaming strange lands?

While she cycled I struggled to be born.
Mother labored, annoyed
at the doctor & my father who were
discussing baseball statistics. Later,
Dorothy got her contributor's copy
of *National Geographic*.

Her story, her photos, & fuck JOL & MOW.
Was she perhaps a spy? Maps that show "new lines
on the furrowed face of Europe," and her route
along rivers and borders, her sudden decision
to jump ship and cycle from Geneva to Trieste,
then in Vienna a letter saying come to Krakow –

6

A letter from Jack – who's Jack? A friend, a lover? She carries
just a rucksack and a Rolleicord camera, her stories are light-
hearted but. Poles are finally able to speak their own language,
yet remnants of the Great War are everywhere, shell-torn
buildings, roofless houses, shattered gallant former officers
who flirt with her. It's 1939, doesn't anything in her clever red
head tell her, watch out, here we go again, I think she *is* a spy –
she observes the Poles' attempts to defend themselves, pays
attention to how independent they are, notices the Jews in
black satin caftans single corkscrew curls fur-trimmed velvet
hats. The abundance of Jewish life surprises perhaps repels her.
She has the genial Anglo-Saxon anti-Semitism of the 30's.
There are so many Jews. When she gets off the train the first
things she sees are soldiers and Jews. Unreal she says. An
operetta. Jack has met her at the train station and hands her
into a droshky, so lightly balanced on its springs it seems to
float on the cobbled streets, the horse's hooves echo, Jack
whisks her away.

7

Romantic, exotic, quaint. Meanwhile my mother struggles to
birth me through the early morning hours, I twist, my wee
collarbone splinters, for weeks afterwards she cries is afraid to
wash me change my diaper feed me although she does all
these things through her tears I am her first born in a thunder-
clap a lightning storm.

8

When I was young I wanted a life like Dorothy's for myself.
Mother and Dorothy seemed like opposites, alike only in that
spunk bred out of the Depression, their jobs in factories or as
typists, their saved up pennies splurged for a third-class steamer
ticket or a wedding dress. Yet Mother used to ride a motorbike,
she took dares, wore slacks, flew with Daddy in this open plane.
She threw away her unencumbered life for me.

9

Turquoise train cars roll with purpose
& design though they are smooth
windowless steel without drivers
they communicate somehow

though they are blind they
sniff me out turn as one
panicked I abandon the flivver
start running between train cars

what would Nancy Drew do
she had a flivver like mine
for a while I was free as Dorothy
on her bike the air whipping past me

10

Dorothy is sardonic about Jews, Gypsies, Catholics & their
superstitious ways. She likes the Saxons of Transylvania.
They are clean, frank, worship properly in a gothic Evangelical
church, speak High German, waltz, live in solid houses.
Oh Dorothy, something is about to happen, don't you feel it?
Didn't you see it in the oil fields of Ploesti? Didn't you smell it
in the Jewish market place where people are eager to sell a
single shoe, a saucepan with a hole in it, where dresses and suits
hang like scarecrows on the synagogue fence?

11

The Cincinnati Reds won the Pennant in 1939, lost the World
Series to the Yankees. Armco Steel called back the men from
layoffs; the country suddenly needed lots of steel.
My collarbone healed; I was spoiled & crabby.
Mother put up tomatoes & beans.
Dorothy, whooping & singing, free-wheeling down the
mountains, remembered the droshky, how it skimmed the
cobblestones, the filigreed arch over her horse's neck, that
beautiful iron-gray high-stepping horse.

The Penelope Interview

(We caught up with Penelope just prior to the opening of her new exhibit of fiber art, "Seduced by Color." See it now at the Ithaca Center for the Arts.)

I. Tell me a little about your background – where you grew up, your artistic influences...

P. I was a tomboy in Sparta, and that's the worst possible place for anyone interested in art. You already know the high points of my life. I married Odysseus when I was 15. My rude ungrateful son Telemachus was born the following year. Troy took my husband; I was 17. Ithaca became my home, my legacy, my trap. In that sense, I suppose, Ithaca influenced my artistic development but it was a backwater. You saw very little new in Ithaca.

I. Fiber art was virtually unheard of in 1200 BCE.

P. My invention. If I may say so, it was remarkable, since I had to handle all the practicalities of life alone. I kept the kingdom for my husband and for Telemachus, not that he appreciated my efforts. Then there were the suitors.

I. About the suitors –

P. Now *there* was artistic influence. Necessity. So I began weaving. But the more involved I got in Laertes' shroud, the more interested I became in questions of form and material – I became far less concerned with the political questions that the weaving solved. I began to see choices, possibilities. At first I used standard-grade linen, but on unweaving the shroud one night I thought – why not introduce some color? Why not use a wider range of material? That's when I wove in some barbed wire –

I. Excuse me. Barbed wire. Invented in America –

P. Oh please. I'm a fiction. Eurydice's invention. No, not Homer's work – it is so odd that people of your time don't see that *The Odyssey*'s main characters are women, and that the poem is written with a woman's sensibility. Consider Calypso, Circe, Arete, Nausicaa, me.

But to continue: I experimented with fish skin, catgut, fern and willow – I used found objects like shells, discarded silks, old maps. My work got more astounding to me with each passing day, but all of it had to be destroyed at night, or so I thought then. I was not having fun.

I. Did you have mentors during that difficult time, people who helped feed your art?

P. You must be joking. I had my suspicious son, a gaggle of frustrated money-hungry hormone-hyped warriors, and my parents who were anxious for me to move on and marry again. Mentors? I did well to keep my sanity.

I. Again I want to ask you about the suitors. Supposedly, you were weaving in full view of them and of the entire court. However did you hide your fiber art?

P. Well, it required some foresight, and a fair amount of secrecy. Most importantly, I could not bear to destroy any more of what was dear to me.

So I kept two looms. My art being boring to watch, especially if you are a savage grasping guest of the palace. While the suitors were devouring Odysseus' stores like the ravening wolves they were, slaughtering heads of cattle and good fat sheep, I simply worked on, then hid my finished pieces in unlikely places, all over the palace. Some in my bedroom, under the olive tree bedstead, some in the workrooms. All those places where the everyday life of the palace went on – the laundries, the kitchens. Highly unlikely that the men would visit there!

And the second loom held dear old Laertes' shroud, which I dutifully unwove each night, until they caught me.

I. Do any of the pieces in this exhibit reflect that terrible time? I gather from what you've said that you are more interested in form than content, but I wonder particularly about the self-portrait that seems to incorporate false fingernails and nail polish sewn to fabric.

P. You're right about the materials I used. Don't try to psycho-analyze the piece. I'm not at all interested in self-involved work, and try not to produce it. That work was not meant to give a pre-packaged impression.

I. And what was Odysseus' reaction when he got home?

P. Its all in the book.

Oh, you mean to my fiber art! He thought it was silly. Woman-ish. He understood the need for Laertes' shroud, he liked that, the ruse appealed to his deceptive nature. And he didn't mind my fake offer to marry whichever of the men could string his bow and shoot an arrow through twelve axes – that just added zest to his ultimate revenge. Odysseus was a splendid and crafty warrior. Otherwise, he could never have returned. I am proud of him. But he has his limitations. Art appreciation being one of them. You may recall that we had spent twenty years apart. I had become who I was. The splendid façade of marital harmony we hid behind could not conceal from my family the fact that my most passionate love was invested in the art I made – not in our son, not in Odysseus. Our last deception was necessary for a peaceful restoration of ordinary life in Ithaca, and it was successful. Odysseus returned to Laertes; Telemachus joined his father and grandfather; they shared war stories and ruled Ithaca.

But let me show you around the exhibit. This one I call "Interior/Exterior." It incorporates casts of body parts, including bits of the suitors. Note my use of scarlet, silver, bronze and golden thread.

TALKING TO STRANGERS

1986

And I hope this will be counted somehow in my defense:
my regret and great longing once to express
one life, not for my glory, for a different splendor.

Czeslaw Milosz

I

Field Trip to the Mill

Sister Monica has her hands full
timing the climb to the catwalk
so the fourth-graders are lined up
before the next heat is tapped, "and no
giggling no jostling, you monkeys!
So close to the edge!" She passes out
sourballs for bribes, not liking
the smile on the foreman's face,
the way he pulls at his cap,
he's not Catholic. Protestant madness,
these field trips, this hanging from catwalks
suspended over an open hearth.

Sister Monica understands Hell
to be like this. If overhead cranes clawing
their way through layers of dark air
grew leathery wings and flew screeching
at them, it wouldn't surprise her.
And the three warning whistle blasts,
the blazing orange heat pouring out
liquid fire like Devil's soup
doesn't surprise her. She understands
Industry and Capital and Labor,
the Protestant trinity. That is why
she trembles here, the children clinging
to her as she watches them learn their future.

Your Language Is Lost at Sea

for Grandma

Since you didn't speak their language
and besides were scared of the big Russian girls
with their oiled black hair and coarse gestures,
silence became your sister, she kept everything
in her heart, in the chill dark, in the hold
of your ship bound for the new country.
Silence was the chosen one in whose deep lap
you buried the Hunkie gutturals and sibilants,
keeping back only the few consonants and vowels
you thought your children would need in Ohio.
So your story trickles down the years: "Say nothing
if you are hungry, tired, poor. And wish to be
nothing as your syllables fall, break the ocean's skin.
With empty hands touch your body,
its boundaries and frontiers. Whoever invades,
hold tight, hold your tongue. Silence will bless
like a sister the tears you keep to yourself."

The Rope

Their voices still wake me
as I woke for years to that rise and fall,
the rope pulled taut between them,

both afraid to break or let go.
Years spilled on the kitchen table,
picked over like beans or old bills.

What he owed to the mill, what she wanted
for him. Tears swallowed and hidden
under layers of paint, under linoleum rugs,

new piled on old, each year the pattern
brighter, costlier. *The kids*
he would say, *if it weren't for*

She'd hush him and promise
to smile, saying *This is what
I want, this is all I ever wanted.*

My Father's Story

The blast furnaces dead, the cities dark,
the iron and ice ringing underfoot
but ringing for nothing, all for nothing,
no light in any house but kerosene,
the Depression a huge fact, a frozen hump
he couldn't get over or around,
the primitive helplessness
of his parents – outraged,
the young man leaves to cut
ice on the pond, 40 cents an hour,
his bucksaw biting deep
into another man's property.
If he can't shape steel
he will sheathe these blocks
in yellow sawdust and lay them up
against the coming heat.
The ice at least will have
its occupation: in July, sweating
his sweat, oozing its wet golden drops
onto the ice house floor.

Steel Poem, 1912

for Kevin

When the mill crept into his bunk-room
beating a fist on his wall

and the sun rose in sulfur
piercing the company house

he dressed with the men
cursing the lard on his bread

the sponge of new steel
waiting for him and his brothers

the shovel and pound
the steel rolling out

and he dreamed of dove-hunting
plump birds hanging like fruit

the soft bones eaten with flesh
how they tempered the heart of the eater.

1920 Photo

Here is Grandpa, who did not want America,
flanked by children, wife and brother,
brother's wife and children. . . . Standing
to one side, a Chinese woman.

How did she get into this picture!
My mother can't, none of my aunts
can tell me, but they are children here,
see their rosy faces. The mustachioed men,
their women proud in white lace blouses,
a solemn occasion . . . and the Chinese woman

in a stiff bright robe, her eyes shining
into mine. Except for her, everyone touches
everyone else, all of them are making it
in America, even if Grandpa cries for Hungary
at harvest-time, even if he is a landless farmer
who shovels slag at the rolling mill.

Even the Chinese woman, who no one alive remembers,
who migrated into my family's picture
like a jungle bird among chickens,
looks happier to be here than Grandpa.

Family Traits

Always one last order
before she released them
from their oven-on-wheels,
the family Ford:
Don't ask for anything.

The children never questioned this.
Their mother's pride was at stake.
They knew better than to wish out loud
for a cold Royal Crown or ice cream,
and if offered anything
even Aunt Mary's noodle pie
they knew how to refuse.

They practiced refusal
sitting on the prickly sofa
watching bars of buttery light
through the Venetian blinds,
feeling brave while their mother's sisters
begged them to eat a little something,
but not relenting until they saw
their mother's discreet nod.

As grown-ups, they notice their hands
are often groping and empty
but they only know how to refuse
and they're still not asking for anything.

2

At Grandpa's wake my uncles sit together,
waiting to be fed. Not speaking yet.
They rest their arms on the long table,
rounding their shoulders under stiff white shirts.

When words come, you out there will hear
only the economy of their sentences:
"That goddam choir." "The Old Man
loved fiddle-music for dancing, you know, *czardas,*
so when Johnny dumped his fiddle on the B&O tracks . . ."
"We should have learned Hungarian, but we got our faces
    slapped
if we didn't talk American." "No matter what he said,
I never talked back." "That damned young priest,
couldn't even say the Old Man's name right."

My uncles share a habit they picked up
from the Old Man: whenever they lose their tempers
they bite their tongues. Today they nearly
bite their tongues in two, hooking the teeth
in the thick dumb muscle
that jerks in their mouths like a bludgeon.

False Teeth

Walking back to her sister's house,
woozy from relief and Novocain,
she nearly trips on the B&O tracks.
Then she sees it. A $20 bill.

Not crumpled. Folded between the ties,
pleated into a little fan, as if arranged
by whatever tooth fairy looks after
30-year old women who lose all their teeth.

When she walks into her sister's and grins,
she scares the baby – her swollen face,
the gums still bleeding, her words clotted
like the cries of an animal –

They think she's gone crazy with pain until
she holds up the money. The men are laid off
again, but she can pay the dentist
what he's owed, she can buy false teeth.

They say, "For every child, a tooth,"
and this is a story for children
whose toothless mother lost
and found and came out even.

Uncle Rudy Explains the Events of 1955

We laid the last course of firebrick
in the big 3-storey kiln when something broke upstairs.
Us brickies on the kiln bottom held our breath
at the first whiff of lime, we knew that stuff
could blind you, burn your lungs.
Each man found another man's hand
before shutting his eyes, so we inched out
that way – like kids, eyes shut tight
and holding hands. Climbed the ladder, finally up
to sweet air, the lime falling like snow
and burning our skin all the way.
That was the winter I found a rabbit
in one of my traps still alive.
The noise he made. "Quit it quit it quit it."
Lord, just like a person. So I quit.

August

Someone hung bronze bells on the saplings
growing from the cellar-hole

at the edge of Mr. Bryant's cornfield.
They rang a little, company to locusts

who filled each cave of trees, a choir
I could step into, walking down the road,

or out of, if I chose. Better
to sit in dust, under the arbor,

pulling down hollyhock blossoms.
Mother lay in the house,

bearing down. My sister's head emerged,
a purple plum. She wore her skin

so like the hollyhock dolls
mother had made all summer:

the blossom a full-skirted gown,
the head a green bud, skewered
by a single straight pin.

Paper Dolls

Shoe-boxes full of them, so helpless
yet haughty, mascaraed eyes
open and distant; the cardboard bodies,
naked except for wisps of peach lingerie,
not like our mother's body, zippered in smocks.

How we made the dolls bow,
imagining the rustle of dresses,
murmuring the names
which were not like our names:
Giselle. Marline. Katrinka.

They could not speak. We spoke for them,
exchanging identities like spies,
settling marriages and dowries,
folding them in outfits labeled "Tennis."
"Lunching at Maxim's." "Caribbean Sail."

We moved into their bodies, divided
the males among us. Until our mother
called us down to set the table,
we could live anywhere, eat what pleased us,
wear electric blue satin and furs.

All Souls Day, 1957

This is the day the poor souls wait for,
it is Christmas to them.
We run into church and out,
saying our prayers aloud and fast,
every set of prayers a ransom
breaking another soul free
from Purgatory's swampy floor.

Slipping between the brass doors,
black uniforms flapping about our knees,
we are raucous crows, but no one stops us.
Spirits drift up to Heaven like soap bubbles,
borne by our Paters and Aves, or by the draft
from the constantly opening doors.

All day, we are diligent about this work:
in the dawn before Mass, during recess,
after school, until the air turns blue
with burning leaves, for so many thousands
of souls are lined up like paratroopers
aimed upwards, poised for a hundred,
a hundred thousand years, waiting
for our prayers to cut them loose.

This is the day we are powerful:
not Sister or Father, not even God Himself
can say no to us, as we command that a murderer
(one who repented before the switch was thrown)
may put by his pain and soar.
Even the atheist Russians must envy us
as their Sputnik circles our little world
and their dog presses his nose to the window
watching our poor souls enter Paradise.

Lessons

Aunt Julie's hands knot and whiten
as she squeezes cucumber slices
handful by small handful
into the pale green bowl.

Called away from the uncles
to help in her hot kitchen,
I am beginning to learn
the woman's part. The man's part

is no better. After his mill shift
Uncle Vernon will stand at the back door,
shaky and black. He likes

cucumber salad, so this is the least
Aunt Julie can do: wringing the slices
as if they are somebody's neck.

The Mill in Winter

Below them, the valley cradles
the mill's dark body which lay
for a decade like a stunned animal,
but now awakens, almost innocent again
in the morning light. A pale disk of sun
pinks the crusted snow the men walk on,
the first thin columns of smoke brush the sky,
and the odors of coke and pickling acid
drift toward them. They taste metal on their tongues
and yearn toward the mill's black heart.
To enter, to shut out the bright cold air
is to enter a woman's body, beautiful
as ashes of roses, a russet jewel,
a hot breath grazing their arms and necks.

Uncles' Advice

My handsome uncles like dark birds
flew away to war. They all flew back
glossier and darker than before, but willing
to be clipped to the mill for reasons
of their own – a pregnant girl,
a business failed, the seductive sound
of accents they'd grown up with –
so they settled, breaking promises to themselves.
This was the time I moped in my room
while the aunts' voices rose through the floorboards
prophesying my life, stews and babushkas.
But the uncles' advice also filtered up
like the smoky, persistent 5-note song
of the mourning dove: get out, don't come back.

Carolyn at 16

Mama and Nana hide behind
the front porch, whispering *money
money* as you swing on the porch
like a ship into Sex Ocean with your slick
exchange student from Ecuador.

His elegant feet flick the porch boards
quick as a lizard's tongue. And his shirt
fluorescing under the street light, white on white!
The living room sighs with applause
for you, honey loaf – the family's capital.

The old women click like sticks
in the tiny rooms stuffed with rosewood,
they trace circles on the wet rims
of old crystal. You on the porch swing,
meant to restore their nice world,

Carolyn, your black hair cloudy, lifting
from your neck in the humid air –
marriageable, he thinks, *virgin*,
but not rich, not *católica*,
and flips his cigarette over the rail.

Carolyn at 20

One hand on the trailer door, one holding
your baby, you turn to watch the oil-rag sun
swipe down the sky. All Middletown knows
the father: string-muscled briar-hopper
your mama says you *chose*; and he's decamped.

You sit like a stump outside town
or hang out the diapers like flags;
you bury the trailer wheels in cement sockets,
oh thorn in your mama's side. Judgment,
she says, that gray streak in your glossy hair,

but standing under the fuming sky,
your son's fist in your hair, you name it:
joy, the dark rooms of your mother's house
exploded at last, the caverns of a man's body
shot with light, as beautiful as you suspected.

Carolyn at 40

When she leaves his house the sun bruising her skin
hurries her toward the car, the safety of leather,
the notebooks clotted with specs
of the "homes" she tries to sell.

Leaning into the car mirror, she pushes back
a stiff wing of hair the same sure way
she pushed his head back, baring his throat.
He's not much older than her son.

Carolyn shuffles photos of ranches
and handy-man specials, dealing them
like tarot cards: the farm means *love*,
the condominium means *you'll never go back*.

Brochures spill to the floorboards.
She crushes one, wiping her hands
of his body's lingering scent.
It's late, she has to get out of here.

What Mother Wanted for Me

> *What then do I want?*
> *A life in which there are depths*
> *beyond happiness. . . .*
> Louis Simpson

A house like hers, nicer
but not so nice as to be strange.
Richer sooner. Younger longer.
More of my teeth in my head.

A man like hers but
no midnight turns. No layoffs
or salt tablets for the heat, no milk
for the ulcer. No accidents.

Children. Not so many.
Love that would know
how to make a bed and lie in it,
no complaints. Love that could eat

whatever was put on its plate
or stand before its grave-site
and stare without flinching at the stone
long before it carried dates.

Steelmark Day Parade, 1961

Blondes are everywhere – on floats,
watching from sidewalks, blond cops
joking with tow-headed kids, pale
high school bands with glinting horns.
My dark-haired visitor from Chicago
asks if the town exposes brunettes at birth,
and what we have done with our Negroes.

The strawberry, copper and yellow hairs
on everyone's heads blur in the sun,
doubling and tripling the flash
of steelmarks stamped everywhere
on the floats just passing from view.
This steelmark is heraldic, new,
a steel-blue brand honoring the men
who make steel. Everyone loves it.

"But really, where *are* the Negroes?"
he asks again. Not here, not yet,
they don't exist in 1961. Even the word
Black lies hidden in old wood houses,
cooped in dim regions between the railroad tracks
and the Pentecostal church, forbidden
to make steel or wear the steelmark
branded on the hard-hats of the town's blond men.

Consumers

Suddenly they were all rich.
Pickups bloomed with trailer hitches,
outboard motors shone in the driveways.
They'd convoy to the lake, swim and grill steaks
until the men left for 4 to 12's.

Daily, the women had
something new to talk about,
but the chromed machines
purring in their kitchens
and the strangeness of old rooms
masked with stiff brocade
unnerved them; frowning, they fingered
drapes and carpets like curators.

They began to pack fat onto bellies and thighs
as if preparing for a long journey on foot
through a frozen country, a journey
they would have to take alone and without provision.

Brother Plans to Move

If he can choose, he'll dance out of town,
his wife tossing her hair, gold earrings
down to her shoulders catching the light,
his children robed in scarves like flames,
all of them in carnival masks, tossing pennies
to the stay-at-homes, and it won't matter
when bits of the mill struggle for breath and stir
and mutter after them as they wheel out of town.
They'll slap the dust from their sandals
on the "Welcome to Middletown" sign.
If they look back, the town will turn to salt.

Your Idioglossia

for my sister

Our private language had to stop,
I can see that now, they had to
separate us – you to speech therapy,

me to wait for you in the cobbled yard
without toy or book, watching
the water's slow drip from fountain

to stone basin where the orange carp
flashed and retreated. I understood
it was my fault no one understood

a word you said, but I was glad to keep you
in our puzzle of language, I was keeper
of your tongue – our parents had to

find the door, knock, *ask* to be let in.
Do you remember any of those words?
Sometimes odd syllables swim up and I catch

a glimpse of bright enameled scales,
the pure verb, a long muscle of orange –
then water closes over my head.

Family Dream

I am rolling around on the big bed with Uncle
Jimmy. It's okay, it's only sex, the rest
of the family crowds into the bedroom, laughing
about new babies, new wine. "Bulls Blood"
says Uncle Rudy. Suddenly I remember:
only two lbs. of lamb in the kitchen,
to feed so many! I run down to the kitchen,
start cubing the lamb for goulash.
Mother comes in and tells me to do
something with noodles. "More lamb!" I say.
"Send a cousin out for lamb."
"And who will pay?" asks Mother.

We gaze at each other.
This is a money matter, this is serious
business. I wake up, ravenous.

After Watching a Film about Cargo Cultists

Like everyone else, they want to be happy,
have simply confused cause with effect.
They surmise that
if you build airports you get goods:
cartons of canned soup, boxes of music, pictures that talk;
so they spend their days not working for wages
but in contriving sham runways
marked with bits of bark and paper lanterns
meant to lure the American god,
the giver of gifts, down from the sky.

In the movie the men stand with hands enmeshed
in the wire-link fence surrounding
one of our army's airports, a look of longing
on their faces as they gaze at our planes,
a look I've seen before on faces
in Ohio shopping malls, at family reunions
when the California cousins pass around photos
of white yachts on blue water. . . .
a shared belief that somewhere
in the guts of expensive machines
lives that soft animal, peace-of-mind.

How to catch and keep it
is the problem, how to fool the god
so he'll descend and be captured,
so the soul residing in the roar of the new
power mower or in the twinkle
of the swimming pool's blue eye
will enter the faithful
like the Pentecost dove
blessing and burning
transforming the world.

Grandma's Hands

She flattened my hand on the table,
teaching me loss. Castle Kamen assembled
again under her tracing fingers:
here, the footbridge arched over a troll
who beckoned her, having lured
the soul of her sister, dead at eighteen,
a blank of braids and white dresses;
there, the dining room trembled; the hungry ghost
beat her little shoes against the shelves,
the crockery swayed, "but when we look,
is nobody there." And the chicken run
soaked with blood, where her father
leveled his gun at gypsy women, laughing
as they dropped fat hens from under
their full skirts – over all these fallen places
she shook lost harvest smells,
the sweet Hungarian pepper.

Days in her Ohio kitchen, in the ordinary rooms
where tables hid in oilcloth, in her garden
where St. Francis smirked among white-painted rocks,
her hands gave shape to the air.
Her crooked fingers,
one thumb nail-less from a parrot's bite,
made me yearn for another world
that breathed in roots of the grass not here,
not in Ohio where nothing ever happened.

_____ II

The Persistent Accent

Until the grave covers me, on foreign soil
I shall remain Hungarian.

Hungarian folk song

Because this fat old lady
has exactly the voice
of my dead grandma,
I find myself
trailing her through the supermarket
as she complains to her friend
about the Blacks, the kids, the prices,
age, disease, and certain death,
and I'm seduced
by that Hungarian accent
decades in this country can't diminish,
and I see the smoky fires
of the harvesters, a golden-braided girl
fetching their dinners of peppers and lamb,
and I follow her
through the aisles,
wanting to lay my face
between her hands,
to ask her for a song.

Father on the 40-Meter Band

At peace again, the company upstairs,
my father sits in his basement flicking switches.
Triangular dials glow obediently green
as the stacks of receivers and transmitters,
sheathed in gray metal, stutter to life.

Bunched wires furred with dust may seem
to spring like anarchy from the backs
of his machines, but that is illusion:
he is in control, his hands soldered the wires
and planted the tall antenna for catching voices.

Soon he will call "CQ" into the night,
and a stranger will answer.
"Do you read me? How's my signal?"
All afternoon my father suffered his family,
the stories of their lives. He does not care

for stories, he is interested in signals
clear or faint, anyone's voice homing in
over the miles. Upstairs, I watch
the herringbone pattern of his voice
on the TV: my father, talking to strangers.

Jealous Wife

1

We built the house with a blank wall
facing north: no openings for storms
or winter wind. I want to live
like that wall, blind to how you see yourself,
or be the dead and shining moon,
swollen hunter's moon in the bare elm,
or even less: shadows cast on a kitchen window.

2

Here lies the full skeleton of a deer.
You hope the hunter dropped him
with one shot, though you know
it didn't happen that way.
The delicate puzzle of footbones,
precise as a map, tells you
he climbed here to die.
You pity the animal who dragged himself
into this alder stand.
But everything reduces to sexual bones:
gates that swing open, glittering, underground.

3

Bad dreams, bad dreams, a woman outside
points to our door, but it is locked.
The red chair holds me in a stiff arm,
smoke rises under the lampshade, my hand
unravels the light gathered in a wineglass.
This is fear, it should be anger,
my face should rise like the moon,
searching outside, the policeman's beam
shining into your car.

Finding My Twenty-Year-Old Chicago Diary

1

In the middle of my life I can
look down time's tunnel and find her,
but I can't grab her by the hair
and shake her free from the desk where she works
or writes in her secret journal
when she should be working,
or gazes at the lake "striated like the muscles
on a man's back." She is newly married,
still wonders at sex,
there is no way for me to save her.
She wants poetry and "ordinary human happiness"
and is still young enough to believe
she can have both at once.

2

She watches Lake Michigan freeze solid
ninety-six miles across, the ice green
but sometimes "mimicking the air's no-color,
the waves frozen in attitudes as if about to break."
She is about to break, and I want her back
so I can put my hands again
on the thin cold face that lived in my mirror.
I'd be her good mother before her babies come
and croon a lullaby about giving over
to the wind, bending like the trees
she writes of, bent along the Outer Drive,
their wind-flattened, squat, but vivid forms
an image to her as she bends over her proofsheets:
Adventures in Reading: A Teacher's Manual, Grade 5.

3

Her husband rises, dresses in the dark,
leaves their building eating an apple,
his teeth cracking into white flesh:
delight in the crack of the icy
train platform under his feet.
Under the frozen lake the swelling water
prepares to break free and he plants his feet
on the surface of a world which will yield
to him and to the wife he left in bed
with proof her body is good for something –
he felt the child fluttering
under her skin, the work between them.
She is willing to pay for her choice
while the surge of another life, like the lake
tossing its bones, buries the words deep under:
"plain is a good word, and so is *smear."*

4

As morning comes on, things resume their lives:
the lake leaves the arms of the dark air
and steps once more into its own shape,
trees detach from rocks, mother and daughter part.
Each thing in the dense world of things
says hello to itself, delighted to be
in the light again. But for her the only way out
is down, through black water. If she holds her breath
for fifteen years, she is still living a life,

a body becomes history for the children,
a rib around which their lives accrue,
for in the lived life, nothing is final.
By entering the lake weighted on both hips
she can walk the bottom,
allowing the lake's heavy plate to press her down
until bitterness leaches from her and time lets her rise.

Separations

1.

The last angry word hangs like a cleaver
over the shag carpet, then slices down,
and there is a ravine in the living room floor
dividing husband and wife who gape at each other
from either side.
                At the gulley's bottom
a thin line of horsemen, silent from this distance,
threads its way through pin-oaks and a desultory stream.

2.
The tourists admire the ice floes; it may be
that we are also picturesque: a tired man
with a sore throat, two weeping children,
the seasick mother.
                Our captain says,
"We call it calving when the glacier splits."
And the ice hits the water
before we hear the sounds of that birth.

The Gazebo

Mr. Bryant built the gazebo
their first year together.
Shavings fell from his dovetail plane
blond as a young wife's curls.
He dreamed of her white skin
while the eaves curved under his hands,
and he trained the grape vines
to grow over the sides
and darken the open room.

Mrs. Bryant strung the washlines there,
after she retrained the vines
to grow on a proper arbor.
A gazebo's a good place for laundry
when it rains, and it rains
most of the summer, in Vermont.

I Get Jealous of an Old Home Movie

How sharply I catch my breath –
his movie of Christina skating
red hair flying
as she drifts
among the dead trees
studding the frozen pond,
a fluent bird alive
in the still trunks and branches.
Those images are acid flung in my face
by Jealousy, that useless hag,
who after all these years
can still catch me under the ice
and tie my hair
to the roots of frozen trees
while Christina's skates
cut the ice above me,
indifferent and free.

Hospital Call

The angel hunching on the TV set is bored.
I won't look at her, but can feel
the irritated whir of wings
as I lean over my husband,
watching his thick chest fill and fall,
letting his breath wash my face.
The angel's not waiting for him.
She wants the black man in the next bed,
the one with cold fingers
and no wife to stand over him and pray
the sweat to break from his body.

The angel visits so many rooms like this one –
fluids pumping into bodies, pumping out,
night-sweat and vomit, dank hair spread on pillows –
she likes this taking to be easy.
She wants us to be beautiful and good,
cool as white nightgowns carved in stone.

I want a barroom brawl,
the TV blaring the Steelers score,
the black man banging his glass,
poking his finger in my husband's chest,
while I pull out
the angel's cotton candy hair
by its black roots.

The Ghost

In the darkness my husband could sense it
standing at the foot of the bed, hunched
and hesitant. Then the small sound
of a hand touching coins on the dresser.
"What do you want? Go away!" he said.
He wasn't afraid, just firm, and the sternness
in his voice woke me from a dream:

A woman had wandered onto a road
and was lost where no one wanted her.
The hemlocks pressed her close on either side,
their black hands laced, so she needed
to keep moving toward the one figure
she could see, outlined in light:
a man waving impatiently from the road's crown,
his voice imperious, demanding something.

After the Facts Came Out

Ellen R., the gourmet cook
who secretly melted her flesh back to its bones
must have hated us as we stuffed ourselves
on her marriages of butter and egg,
sweetbreads in velvet sauce,
raspberry hearts melting with sugar.
At table she sat upright watching us eat
her celebrated bouillabaisse; she shaved
dark chocolate curls for our delight,
and when we moaned with pleasure, she would smile.
But at the New Year's buffet
she lifted her long dress over her head –
the skimmed blue-white skin stretched over ribs,
the sharp-edged dish of pelvis, the two scraps
of breast, a presentation for the dinner guests.
Not long after, she left her husband, gave up cooking,
went back for her Ph.D. and the life of the mind.

Book Circle

In February, in Ramona's house
with its authentic stenciled walls,
they gathered to discuss
Charles Williams' Anglican ghost stories.
Meanwhile, little sexual brushfires
caught all over the room.
The cold Vermont wind swept under the hall door,
they drew close to the fireplace
and turned to the story in which a woman
meets her Doppelgänger in Cambridge. . . .
and a man changes into lion, serpent, bear. . . .
"Marriage is a burning house,"
Ramona told her guests. All of them
were married, but not to anyone present.
Ramona's voice sounded against the windows,
black diamonds against the night sky.
One of the guests knew she shouldn't be there,
and pulled on her thick gloves. A wasp
which had crawled into a glove gave the sting,
something for her to carry back home.

On Murray Avenue

I don't know the boy who runs
toward me, holding out his arms.
You look so pretty, he shouts,
and grabs me round the shoulders.
I see that only his mind
is young – some mother's hand
still combs his hair, though it's graying,
but maybe he chose the red tee-shirt,
it looks brand-new, and if
my heart were less a closed fist
I would not shudder
out of this sidewalk two-step,
I'd hug him back, tell him
he looks pretty too.

The Golden Ox Cafe

A newspaper clipping from home, headlined
"Duke Morris – Tough Guy, Poetry Lover."

Morris owns and runs
The Golden Ox Cafe in Dayton Ohio.
An ex-boxer, ex-Marine.

He says, "I love poetry
final and foremost in my life.
I love poetry more than I do women."

———————

A friend, a notable writer, got drunk
at my house, lay down on the floor
and cried, "I have no spiritual life."
Then he said he had no character,
for he could not bear to leave his wife
although he loved another woman
and longed to be with her.

———————

Duke Morris believes his poetry
will catch on in a big way once he has died
and will make him immortal.

"I don't want any money," Morris said.
"I don't want to be rich.
"I want everyone to read my poems."

———————

The notable writer thinks that when he is 80
he will be happy again, for then
no one will care who he fucked, only what he wrote.
He thinks of poems extending themselves,
thickening like the rich vines of honeysuckle
behind his mistress' house, and sex
as just a metaphor for writing, and on this point
Duke Morris would probably agree.

———————————

The man who loves poetry more than women
is coming to terms in Ohio, in The Golden Ox Cafe,
wiping down vinyl tables, upending chairs.

He draws the shades, eats some leftover
stew and bread, sets out his workbook
with its marbled cover, picks up his favorite pen.

I'm Calling the Exterminator

I don't know how the raccoon broke into the chimney
but I want it out: alive, dead, whole or in pieces,
poisoned, shot or merely discouraged from its anxious
      scrape scrape scrape
at 3 a.m. in the chimney's hollow behind my headboard.
Imagine its clever worried mask, the quick paws
passing over each other, clawing a space in my life
when I'm helpless and asleep, the stubborn scrabbling of
      the creature
no matter how hard I hit the wall with the baseball bat –
what can it be doing back there? I hear drawers opening
      and closing,
furniture dragged along the floor then dropped. Then,
      muffled curses.

How to Winter Out

Love the land mass, the enclosure
of a continent around you.
Think of yourself as the hot center.

Remember frostbite, how the blood rushes
from hands and feet to save the heart.
Do likewise, pare down to the vital.

Do without color, except the necessary
cardinal on a branch,
a spot of blood on snow, a burning coal.

But dream when you sleep, and dream in color.
Do not tell your lover your dreams
unless he asks. Then embroider.

Otherwise, do not adorn. Make love
without speaking, make love in Spanish,
speak in tongues, but use no names.

III

German Stories

1

Fallen trees, their great trunks fluid with years,
sprawl among the brush and fireweed
or bend as girls do, brushing their hair.
I thrust my hand into a hollow tree
and draw out its sacred name,
the name we must never pronounce,
before the German machine, bristling with order,
comes to scour the woods it loves so much.

2

Early morning
waiting alone on the platform
mist rolling in
as if the past
were a door left open
waiting for the Munich train
its sleek body
enormous windows hiding nothing
no slatted sliding doors
a man's heavy tread
coming up the station steps
he whistles an old marching song

3

A Letter from Munich
Our landlady is kind to me and the children for we look
German. Also, I like to walk across the kitchen floor
barefoot for the pleasure of the scrubbed bleached
wood under my feet. The landlady knows this.
Yesterday she taught me to make plum tarts. We filled

the kitchen with the smells of preserves and burnt sugar. She said
the Jews are *Fliegen*, and are best dealt with – smack! – like *this*.

4

Cats live in the eternal present,
they have no internal clock,
they are like God.

Or like Germans, who have many clocks,
all of them external,
all of them on time,
many of them beautiful, like cats.
Like cats, they have no history,
have always stood on shelves

in shops with drawn curtains
where I stand now with the shopkeeper.
We sway back and forth like figures

on his cloisonné clock. Hansel and Gretel
shuffle on the witch's threshold
while the cat's black tail swings: Tick, Tock.

5

The sudden apparition in the car mirror of a dark Mercedes-Benz
bearing down on us, 80, 90 mph? – headlights blinking, then
around us and gone. *What's happening?* My friend laughs and
smoothes the feathers on his loden hat. "We are not used to speed
limits in Germany – when they put some limit on the *Autobahn*,
this was to us a life without joy, a terrible burden, it depressed the
whole nation. It's different for Germans, we can't be constrained."

6

I could hear it breathing
under the streets, shackled
like a bad dog – the old city,
simmering under the new.
Yesterday a little woman
jostled me in Marienplatz.
I wanted to tear out her throat.
That's the trouble with this country,
its lack of distance,
and not enough faces.
Everyone looks like me.

Two Photographs

Why am I crying over these pictures?
My mother is alive,
my daughter is a beautiful young woman.
But here, each of them
is four again, with the same
soft chin and pale hair, even the same
nervous tic: five fingers stuffed in the mouth.
The feathery wisps of Lisa's hair,
a fragrance like cut grass
rising from Mother's neck. . . .
When Lisa burrowed in my arms,
my pleasure was the same as it was
for Mother when I shoved myself into her,
all those soft arms and legs twined round.
Lisa pretended to sleep so I would carry her
from car to bed, and I dreaded the time
she would not want to pretend.
I remember Mother's hand on mine,
tracing the storybook words
long after I knew their meanings,
and now I wish to hear whatever story
makes them look so sad in these pictures.
What can I do with this longing for that union,
touching their faces, then my own.

Cold Frame

March again, so we pry the cold frame open.
The hinged lid creaks like a knee,
but will hold together one more year.
As we shovel peat moss and clean sand,
I warn my daughter: not too rich a mixture,
or the roots grow shallow.
We pack the light loam down,
her fingers are longer than mine.
She is thirteen and careful
of her breasts, yet has a new way
of rocking back on her heels, like a woman.
As she listens, she plants the seed
in perfect rows; her gray eyes measure
the gaps in the cold frame, measure me.

May Morning

to WCW

Flick, flick, there his line goes again
over the backyards of Pittsburgh:
my neighbor practices flycasting,
leans from his second-story porch,
just misses the tangle of last year's nests
and the peeved sparrows as he spins out the thread,
flirting it over the green bushy banks
where imaginary trout lurk and flash,
hanging in pools under the peony bushes –
oh mingle of hope and desire, fish of our dreams –
while in the backyard burns
that green-broken-bottle color,
deep as the sea, and the scent
of our three brown rivers wafts
over the *sempervivum,* those little
cabbage plants, round as roses.

1066

A great wind, and a voice within the wind:
bed and window, house and child.
A voice hoards the old tongue,
a stone falls into the body's pond:
husband, sleep, north and west.
The fired huts, a blond man buries
bread and welcome, fire and hearth,
heaven and earth, bird and tree.
The old words freeze inside the throat
until love or death melt them
and out they flow, brighter than chivalry,
each word a drop of blood:
bloom knife summer friend.

So come Normans, and come servant
mantle convent feast venison and spice,
come guile and courtesy, come rich come poor,
come change delay escape, come doubt
and villain, chalice, rent and savory.
For a voice is singing to itself
under cliff, under grass:
thrive and thrust, gasp and want,
bride meadow beast bower
loom and stream. Happy or ill,
wise or weak, in full day
or skulking night the deep words rise:
path and way, beginning, end.

Forget Your Life

for Michele Murray, 1933-1974

Forget your life, it's familiar,
a housedress you've grown into
so that it seems your second skin.

Soon, pain will take you by the wrist
down to the river, where your skin
under the sloughed-off dress is fresh again.

Though you have rocked the child today
"for hours . . . and could not write,"
poems like cells divide under your breasts.

Soon, your poems will walk on their own,
holding up lanterns
as you enter the sliding river.

Alternate Universe

I can walk into the rain, turn the corner
at Fifth & Wood & vanish into something better,
something harder, a maple tree for example. . . .
Time curves in & out,
a train crawls along, hauling itself toward Juarez.
Or on a different train, the light slanted for winter
instead of July, what would he have said to me then?
I shake alternatives like snow in a glass globe
& the snow comes down, never the same way twice.
So, the train is bound for Juarez, now there's smoky gold
in the air, the cottonwoods shining, each leaf & stem
connected by a flat twist at the twig, the least wind
shakes the leaves, alternating gold & gray flashes,
but the leaves hold tight to their branches.
I'm dizzy from light brushed on leaves passing by,
the rainfall snowfall summer is quick to flame,
it settles into ash. He is far away,
the door spinning at the corner of Fifth & Wood
lets me enter his world where something else
might have happened at ground level. If I spin
the wheel again he might watch from his room my distant
    windows:
at sundown, each one blazes in turn, then darkens.

Tarantula

Nothing to see here but scrub, just a dirt road like a hot held breath
between El Paso and Chandelar, then in front of us,
a tarantula shedding his skin. In the grip of the one beautiful thing
he knows how to do.
The harmless and stout, the hairy and slow
tarantula leaving behind his replica,
exact to the last hair and spot.
This is hard work, he peels himself out, comes out soft and damp,
the pincers curved, pale ivory. Nothing
here but cactus, cholla that jumps at you, ocotillo like little whips,
still trembling, dropped from someone's hand. He could die now,
soft as he is. Watching him leave his body. To have a new body.
The distance between the shell turning to ash
and the tentative flex of his legs,
his slow walk away toward nothing we can see –
a line burning or the horizon, a thread of dust.
Heat carves the silence toward belief
in things unseen – this shroud of old skin
under my fingers.
To slip out of your body, to drop it like an old shirt.
To live, a tarantula must be hard and dry, and now he is,
and gone, blent into the pale dirt, gone before.

World Without End

These insane layings of eggs by the thousands,
clear jellies clinging to the undersides of myriad leaves,
and in the streams and oceans, millions of clusters more,
the hordes eating their way southward through the trees,
or being eaten, but there's a plenty for food,
a plenty to live and breed more. Don't you tremble
at that fecundity? The mindless swell and burst,
and each like each like each. What kind of God desires
such multitudes. Stacked like cordwood on the streets in Delhi,
each a beloved soul. But oh
the raw cries of my father, the night his mother died.
My mother, who can see longer and harder than anyone,
now trying to ease him down. The deaths of the many
are nothing to me. When the sirens warn, I want
everyone I love gathered with me on a high mountain
where we start over, all of us saved by a miracle
because we are mild, intelligent and happy in our work.
But even God can't stop us
from standing on the quarry's edge, daring who will dive
into that black water first,
the insane laying of eggs, the thousands, the millions,
my father wrapped and dying in my mother's arms.

Aphasia

for my father

Because scared, because of *have to earn a dollar,*
because for every thing you earned, Granddaddy sat
on your shoulder saying "You're the lucky one,
if you fell into the shithole you'd come up
with a gold piece in your mouth," because traduced,
laughed at, lied to, because you trusted only your hands
and the perfect ribbons of steel rolling out of the mill,
because you never trusted words but filled a house
with the static of stockpiled things, every gadget,
every stick of furniture a barrier to the threat outside,
because you never felt at home in this world
of jokes and silences, because now you think "death"
but say "black feather," here is a garden:
pass your hand over the face of this thing you've forgotten,
this "flower." Whatever you name it, so it will be.
Hello or Forgive Me. I Loved You. Good-bye.

Dark Trail

I wasn't lost; no one could get lost
on such manicured trails, but without a moon
and caught between the party's and the house's lights
I stood inside the heart of a tree or maybe
inside the sky: I could have been suspended
anywhere, feet moving over – not on –
pine needles blowing down; whatever was left
between feet and head was probably
my body which ignited, a luminous raft,
a dream of flying or floating face down
hair adrift in the pool's gel.
It's good to die a little.
Nothing is taken away. If you and I
were together again on the paddle boat,
we could fly our dragon kite, letting it
follow the boat attached by the thinnest wire.
Lovely to tug on the line, to feel it strong,
tensed to break away. Pluck it,
you hear music higher than wind in these trees
burning their incandescent inward lights.

UXB:
POEMS AND TRANSLATION

1991

The Furies

1

How often I'd wanted the woman dead.
When I married her son a *furor teutonicus*
possessed me and I dreamed for months of slitting
the woman's throat or driving her before me,
cutting into her soft corrupt body with a whip.
Her smallness, especially the smooth manicured hands,
drove me to frenzy. I had often heard the woman's son
recount his beatings at those hands, or his finding her
passed out on the floor, the smear of her mouth as she cursed
his father, the whiskey, her high-heeled shoe
coming down on his skull with a crack.
And so I rejoiced and was glad when we were called
to the old woman's side, the final breakdown at last.
The day swung between sun and driven snow.
Gilt and scarlet flags flapped over the used car lot,
and in the mazes of streets, deep shadows. And in the home,
on the half-lit board of the woman's brain,
more lights pulsed out. The roads the alleys the footpaths
blackened forever. She was wholly in the moment,
no past or time to come. If evil is good's absence,
if faith is the absence of knowledge, then she
was all faith. I could not speak of evil, that nullity.
Her body layered in house-dresses, floppy and loose.
A moat between herself and herself.
Her terror was real, when she felt it.
This was left of her: the delicacy with which
she lit a cigarette and waved away the smoke.
Her smiles loosed from her mouth, something dangerous,

not grounded, words floated in chaotic liquid.
I regarded her with sick fascination. Watched
the genteel veneer boil away. Thought
of bad stories, the worst one, the one when the one
you love best does not die but changes, is emptied.
I found myself packing her sweaters and sachets
as if I loved her; not for her sake,
for the sake of the woman she never was.

2

Fear and loathing
in equal parts,
no running from it.

The Nazi within me
wants her gone
up the chimneys.

My fault she's
a rankling tenant
in my head.

Put shut to it
stop sucking it
sore tooth in its socket

scab picked at, bled
and scabbed over again.
Let her be

whatever she is,
so I instruct myself.
But she's not mine

not mine to forgive.

3

To let her go in peace.
To know she only gave
as good as she got
what she had to give:
yardsticks broken
on her son's back,
fumbles under the covers
for the frozen child
in the dark.
She hurt as she was hurt.
Not to excuse her,
to see her
as one woman
in a sequence of broken women.
She's far gone now.
To let her know
that with her son and me
she was stopped.

Custody of the Eyes

I shouldn't be watching the old bum
in jeans and yellow shirt who shuffles
sideways, crab-like, who flicks out
his hand like a feeler and hits
his mark most of the time, but
I do watch, ashamed and fascinated.
What a psychologist he is,
ignoring the beauty with her bell of bright hair
but stopping a round, bespectacled boy;
he gets his change and moves out of my range.

As usual, I'm pulled two ways –
since deep looking is what love demands,
am I bound to see what is,
or were those Dominicans right
who taught me custody of the eyes,
by which they certainly meant "When you
must walk down Bourbon Street, don't look
at that world, don't look don't look,"
but which I took to mean a kind of charity,
with each of us deserving a private shell
that no one else may reach into;
                              that is, custody
of the eyes as the blessing I had felt in Chicago, eighteen
and a stranger there. I walked through Grant Park as if
invisible; in public, but for the first time no one knew
me or my folks, I could look out
but not be seen, I had never felt so free.
But once in a German restaurant a woman
stared at me eating dinner, apparently absorbed

by my outlandish table habits, and I felt
violated until I looked into her face
and saw nothing there, or at most a placid vacancy.
Somehow, this was worse than avid regard, and for that moment
at least I would have welcomed curiosity as appetite
to understand, and I wished that she could see
me, who she was looking at so blankly.

Truth

Germans only tell the lies that they believe,
and I believed it when I said
"I'm mostly Hungarian," or "American

mostly," if anyone asked. Really I'm half
German, father's side. My mother's mother's
maiden name *was* Singhoffer, but she was *born*

in Hungary, you understand. I was born in 1939
(that is the truth) the beginning of good years
to be anything but German. And the family felt

Hungarian, even Daddy's relatives. After the war
all the aunts and uncles danced to only Gypsy
music at their weddings, told ancient jokes

about the Krauts. Here's one of my father's:
"Either they wear boots and kick your ass,
or they kneel down to lick *your* boots."

Enroute

Who will give me permission?
The railroad guards who rifled my bags, looking for bombs?
The man who retrieved the stale cookies I threw in the trash,
        who ate them methodically, one by one, like a man
        taking his medicine?
Will the train conductor locking the doors
        of my first-class compartment give me permission?
Or the third-class passengers flattened against the locked doors,
the robed Patriarch extending his hand for my kiss,
the black market currency changer who tells me, "You Americans
        are God's favorites,"
the veiled woman outside running, baby on one hip, balancing
        a basket on her head, running toward the moving train,
or the little girl, weighed down and running behind her mother,
        will they also refuse me permission?

Part of the Question   (Aichinger)

The water is high on the square,
the air still rises in bubbles,
but what they sing
no longer gets through to me.
The fish circle the church doors,
who will answer me:
Shall I go into the mountain
or into the house with those
who love me,
and what of the distant view,
the crunch of all the footsteps
once again?
How black my land becomes:
only deep below
time writhes green.

Snow People (Aichinger)

I don't mix easily
with strangers of snow,
of coal, turnips, wood sticks,
I do not touch them
as long as they are cheerfully resplendent,
some with more expressions
than one.
Then when the coals
and the turnips fall,
buttons, button plackets,
the red-lip ribbons,
I watch stiffly
and without a sound.
I do not rush to help.
Perhaps they speak
Milanese
better than I,
that's not come to light.
And that's why silence,
until this light
has taken them lightly
along with everything that hides there
between Milanese and Milanese,
including me as well.

To My Grandmother (Aichinger)

The double doors
into Modena Park,
the question
concerning origin,
concerning religions,
Salesiander Street,
the wife of Major Schultz,
the wife of Excellency Zwitkowitsch,
the fright,
the humility,
the dependence,
Miss Belmont,
the refuge,
the strange corridor,
the gate
that flies open,
the mad dog,
don't be afraid,
it is white
still small
and runs past.

Soldier Stories

Great-uncle Alfred was pleased to ride
with the Hussars and fight for the Kaiser.
He liked the flashy uniform, he pierced
a gold ring through his ear for luck,
which failed him east of Budapest where trenches yawned
and stretched and swallowed him. Alfred spent
the next ten years in Grandma's house howling
at night. When Grandma warned the local girls
to stay away from her brother, Alfred went back
to Hungary, brought home a village girl
and had a life of hitting both her and the bottle.

My German cousin Heinrich, on the other hand,
feigned madness in '44. He'd knock himself
so hard in the head he'd pass out
whenever an *Offizier* came by conscripting
fresh blood for the Russian front. Heinrich
kept falling to the ground, grunting and frothing,
and so he made it safely home to Osnabrück
where he shot dramatic photos of an Allied bomb attack
on the village church. He cropped and hung these pictures
in the pet shop he opened after the war, and to annoy
the neighbors he flew the American flag.

About my brother off the coast of Vietnam
there's nothing to tell, no tragedy or comic turn,
only a curtain he keeps pulled around those years
as if within that cubicle lay his own white-sheeted body.

The Driven Out: May, 1945

Long trains deported people to the east.
Then different people fled on foot, deported west.
The difference was that some of these would live.

These, for example: two young and one old woman
and a child in arms they pass to one another.
Four in an ocean of people with their valises,

satchels and carts, all of those who had the luck
to crawl out from the wreckage, to be driven
west. It's hard for them to stay together – if one

or the other relieves herself, she must step out of line
behind the blasted trees while the straggle pushes on –
it is easy in the dark to lose your place – or the child

needs nursing, or the old woman falls down. Don't be
afraid for them. No one will sprinkle their bodies
with quicklime. This little group will reach Hamburg

and an uncle's unbombed house. Years later they'll remember
walking through the deep dark, an old man's voice calling
through the wavering line of people, he had lost a wife

or daughter, "A-del-a," he called. "A-del-a." His
rough clothes, his hands to the open hole of his mouth.

Foundling (Aichinger)

Foisted off to the snow,
not named before angels,
no bronze, no refuge,
not presented to the fairies,
only hidden in caves,
their signs deftly
erased from the forest maps.
A crazed fox
bites and warms him,
favors him quickly with his first caresses
until, trembling and tormented,
he goes off to die.
Who helps the child?
The mothers
with their old fears,
the hunters
with their fake maps,
the angels
with their warm feathered wings
but without orders?
No sound,
no wings in the air,
no shufflings on the ground.
But come again then,
old crazy helpmate,
drag yourself back to him,
warm him, if your predator's paws
    are still warm,
because except for you no one comes,
be sure of that.

Upended Monument

There's a bronze horse
in Cologne, a blown-up horse,
a horse's ass sticking out
of the earth, tail flowing
heroically. One testicle
is painted orange, the other
a bright yellow and it is
as if the horse had dived
deep underground, burying head
and forequarters. Some want
to restore the horse, reseat
the rider. Others say,
let him be, let him trot and gallop
under there, as well as he is able.

Old View (Aichinger)

I've grown used to this window
and the snow falling through my eyes,
but who followed the lost ones
through the open garden gate,
who sealed the fate of what was there,
the rain barrel
and the moon as moon,
each frozen blade of grass?
Who swung before the morning
until the ropes cracked,
who put a wax hand on the kitchen window,
who settled down in whiteness
and took me as I am?

Event at Freiburg: July, 1990

In spite of its stone
the cathedral seemed light,
a glasshouse or birdcage,
the steeple a lacy iron cage,
and whatever her reasons
she wanted to fly from there.
Whatever glittered on the distant hills
wasn't enough to keep her.
The angels did not bear her up.
Nor did the gargoyles, gaping half-men
and devil-dogs on their haunches,
extend their claws for her.
The two worlds turned aside.
She left no trembling on the air
and on the cobblestones her body
barely raised the sheet thrown over it.

Night of Judgment (Aichinger)

For what should come to light
other than patches of snow,
swords on the edge of childhood,
and toward the forest
the boughs of apple trees
that the moon washed black,
the chickens that are counted.

November Morning: Augsburg

He came back empty-handed from the bakery.
"Closed...it's a holiday," he said. "Todestag."
Day of the Dead. Through the parted curtain,
the morning deep in mist, we watched the fog
drag itself over to the trees
where it uncoiled, and in one tree
a ragged crow flapped damply down
and disappeared, the other trees
splayed their hands but vanished
under the fog's invisible weight.
The morning cowered in a helmet of smoke,
the house opened to remembrance fingering
its blind way to sit at our breadless table.
Breath touched our cheeks and withdrew,
sucked back finally by the day which finally broke.

Winter Answer (Aichinger)

The world is made of stuff
that demands consideration:
no more eyes
to see white meadows, no ears to hear
the whirl of birds in branches.
Grandmother, where have your lips gone
to taste the blades of grass,
and who smells heaven to the end for us,
whose cheeks are still rubbed raw
on the village walls today?
Haven't we found ourselves
in a dark forest?
No, Grandmother, it's not dark,
I should know, I have lived a long time
with the children on its edge,
and it is also no forest.

A Visitor

She calls herself Ella,
but I think she's Josephine,
mean and club-footed,
who used to pinch me
when Mother wasn't looking.
Josephine's thread of a mouth,
needles and pins in her chignon,
("But we must be nice to Josephine
who's crippled and plain and
earns her own living")
and her foreign house smelled
of cabbage and her awful cats,
the Father with bright bulbous nose,
the small terrified sister.
But Ella (she says
her name is)
comes visiting, comes carrying
a great spray of lilac
wet with rain, those blue stones
of eyes that blink out
when she grins, a shudder, milk
curdles, I can feel my teeth
loosen, she'll open her bag
and sling me over her shoulder
like the föhn wind coming
over the Alps, there's a lump of coal
for the stocking and a switch
to switch me with.
She says her name is Ella,
lilac fills the room,

and I want to ask her
"What did you do in the war?"
and I wish I had a chicken bone
to hold out to her
and pretend
that's my finger.

Face from a Newsreel

Pity him from this distance,
the young soldier,
his flat unexceptional face,
his mouth swearing the oath,
the shadow of what may be
recognition as he seems to
understand what he is saying.
You can almost see
his words fly
from him and settle
on a fluted stone column:
the words once said
cannot be called back:
funereal, mocking, the word
become flesh, the sworn man's
fealty, a hunched black shape.
A picture from the deepest
part of his brain parades before him:
hearth-fire glinting on swords,
the hard handclasp of brothers.
To break his word would break
a part of himself.
The terror of words,
more than the sign for the thing,
the Thing itself, the lie
that murders a part of the world.

Timely Advice   (Aichinger)

First of all
you must believe
that day will come
when the sun rises.
But if you do not believe it,
say yes.
Secondly,
you must believe
and with all your might
that night will come
when the moon rises.
But if you do not believe it,
say yes,
or nod your head submissively,
they'll buy that too.

Correspondence (Aichinger)

If the mail came at night
and the moon
shoved insults
under the door:
they would appear like angels
in white raiment and would
stand silent in the hall.

Train Platform: Munich to Dachau

1

Two men, doubtless brothers, both huge
and with the same blank judicious face,
slump on a baggage cart. Near them
a decapitated deer, tied
to another cart. Sag of heavy meat,
a pool of blood widening
on the station floor. Pay
attention, hisses the mind, a lesson here.
It's true, in Munich's Hauptbahnhof
death's uniforms rise quite naturally,
the oiled machine of metaphor
glides easily. How easily
the images align: Aztec priest
in cope of human skin, Carthaginian children
rolled into fiery pits, and this commonplace scene:
just hunter's meat and dull round faces.

2

Dachau is a village known
for its fine views and 18th C. chateau.
A German on holiday inquires
of his dining companions, "Why
do these Americans visit the Camp?
What is it they hope to see?"

3

Early April, 1945; soon the war would be over. Some citizen of Dachau, an amateur photographer, leaned from his balcony early that morning. The sky was still gray; a slight drizzle fell. He saw walking in the street below his rooms a scraggly line of people. He got his camera, knelt behind his lace curtains (the edges show in the pictures) and took three photographs. Three: not one. Careful and deliberate, he recorded what he saw.

One: We see people walking; many are draped in blankets or rags that look, from this distance, like prayer shawls. No faces.

Two: We see a group of fifteen prisoners and, to one side, an armed guard. All the prisoners are stooped; one is humped, as if he carries a burden on his back, under the blanket which drapes him. The street is slick with rain; the figures are reflected in the street.

Three: We see many more people and we also glimpse the balcony from which the photograph was taken. A fine house is in the background – smoke puffs from the chimney, there are carved gables and windows. We see women in this group of prisoners. Some of them wear high-heeled shoes; their legs look white and bare.

4

What do we hope to see? Carmelite nuns
live near the site of Barracks 26,
where the priests and ministers were stacked.
I think the sisters hope to see nothing;
they contemplate how blood and the empty mind
desire to converge and with their prayers
they refuse that coupling.
After the war the poets said,
"no poems about the camps," and
they were right, but still I hope
if not for an image, perhaps
for a small composition to place
against the blank-eyed brothers
back on the platform in Munich. I hope
to see again the young couple from Bremen
who struggled with their infant in his stroller,
rolling it over the difficult white stones
which cover the acres of Dachau. They pushed
the stroller from Jewish shrine to Catholic shrine,
then they stopped at the Carmelites' door.
They saw bright scraps of cloth fluttering from trees
in the courtyard. "What does this mean?"
they asked each other, not being Catholic
or Jewish, but merely German,
young, and of a mind to understand.

In Which Names (Aichinger)

The name Alissa,
the name Inverness,
when and
from which desert borders
carried here,
through which orders,
orders of monks, orders of sisters,
long or lengthways
and where to, where not,
how lasting,
how wasteful
with circled walls,
under winter suns
in torn-open trenches,
ramparts, cradles
with fires, ringlets,
oh names, names,
at least with you two
I am not christened
and am not to blame.

Thirty-One (Aichinger)

I let myself go with pleasure
and I take the thirty pieces of silver with me,
if someone gives them to me,
around my neck
so we can swing back and forth,
we thirty-one,
and so I hear them clinking still
in their gunny-sack
until they're out of the world.
So I, when my tongue stiffens,
still know with my naked ears
the voice that commands you all:
Begin once more!
So then I am happy.

Cave

Sometimes a cave is a passage
something's always coming in
or leaving; it's a bon marche
where customers debark and train
their flashlights on each uncoupled
colorless thing: white toad, tokay
or centipede; the bleached blind fish.
Living without light, these rarely breed
and hardly eat. They are
witnesses to how little you need.
Sometimes a cave huddles
in the dark like a priest you whisper to,
or it's a mouth that hangs dumbly open,
it's a blackness in the spaces between trees
mantling your house like the hawk
which mantles its clutched mouse.

Words of Comfort to a Man Who Stayed in Bed Twenty-Three Years and Then Got Up   (Aichinger)

I say, rejoice
in the seconds
along the edge of the bed,
again I say to you,
rejoice
in the name of the city
Newcastle-upon-Tyne,
the sheep shearing
which you watched
so bravely,
in the new breed
which makes you
superior to pigs,
more than superior,
in the pretty whistles
from Scotland,
back and forth,
don't stand like stone
in the morning,
rejoice.

Rock and Roll

Four of us sit around the lamplit table.
The priest and his wife, our friends,
glow like icons.
After grilled meat and bottles
of Serbian wine, this calm...
then Creedence Revival rolls on the river
over the PA system
and my husband and I are up
and dancing, not, for the moment
thinking it strange to rock and roll in
the only Serbian restaurant in Hildesheim, West Germany,
maybe the first Chicago dirty boogie circa 1957
ever danced there. "A great song,"
we huff, and applaud each other.
Our friends smile; they are still as Byzantine saints.
Nothing surprises them any more; what can be stranger
than history? It's not just that we are Americans, and
predictably crazy. The two of them shouldn't have escaped
but they did; we ought never to have met
but here we are. This poem is not about forever.
It's the handfuls of weeds the priest picks for his wife and me
as we walk back to his church through fields that were bright gold
but now are pale under the moon; it's contraries
embracing each other, a little miracle, like the story
of the town of Hildesheim and its thousand-year-old rosebush
thought by everyone to be long dead until it pushed out
white blossoms and scent onto the rubble of 1945.
Just so, we are blooming, our friends stand with us
together in that moment, we are the world's oldest teenagers,
and rock and roll will never die.

Counted Out   (Aichinger)

The day you
came shoeless into the ice,
the day
both calves
were driven to slaughter,
the day I
shot out my left eye,
but no more,
the day
The Meatcutter's News *said*
life goes on,
the day it went on.

Advice for Nothing (Aichinger)

I

Your first chess book,
Ibsen's letters,
take it away
if you can,
here, take it,
or would you rather drive
the page turners
from your meadow
and after that
Ibsen's goats,
equally white, equally glossy?
There are goats and there are Ibsen's goats,
there's heaven and there's one Spanish gambit.
Pay attention, little one,
there's tinplate, you say,
there's the world,
check whether or not they tell lies.

II

And ask them
what the strange thorax
in the garden should do,
already turned to stone,
the first in this Spring
between the blackberry hedges,
mice
and the wall
by which the water
beats for us,

how it's useful in the garden.
Whether it has need of it,
our garden,
or the garden needs it.

III

And
there have been rumors
about time running out.
Whether this has to do with running,
with races, with times
or with none of the above.

Bound Hands

When he ordered me to untie his hands
and hide the restraints in my bag
I obeyed him instantly, though I knew
it was wrong. He was still strong,
he had already scared the nurses
by wandering into some woman's room
and refusing to leave, saying he'd wait
till Mass started – but when we entered
his room, he lifted his bound hands
and said to Mother, "Look here, Betty,
I would never let them do this to you!"
and to me, "Hide these damned things!" –
so I obeyed him, fast as I'd have flinched
from his soldering iron, and not because
I knew he was dying or that I hated to see
this proud man humbled – I did what he said
without thinking and in fearful haste
(after decades of flaunting my uncurbed will,
as if his poor tongue still could blister me)
like the good German girl I was raised to be.

Sycamore

The neighbor's sycamore, that "filthy tree,"
dropped its scabs of bark on Father's
lush lawn. "He hated that sycamore,"
my sister said as if
it still mattered – still, it mattered.
We laughed but looked over our shoulders.

All the while he lay dying he never
let go: Mother had planted the tomatoes
too early, he wanted them tented,
the side bushes needed pruning,
we were to hire someone – on and on,
as if Spring could not leaf out that year
without the weight of his hand on the earth.

I suppose we expected a mellowing, but he stayed
himself, waking at intervals to chew out lazy nurses
or to curse the food he wouldn't have fed to a dog.
In June, the sycamore's trunk flared aggressive,
mottled and green, annoying as Republicans or
daughters who stubbornly did things wrong: that tree,
an arrogant thing our father could never abide
but had to put up with until he died.

Thirteen Years (Aichinger)

The Feast of Tabernacles
is long past,
the gleam of chestnut trees
lined up at the summerhouse window.
And still in the room
the candle
the religions of the world.

Desert dust under the bicycle wheel.
After this noon
the twilight comes quicker.
Companions
and a green grave,
Rajissa.

We come back every evening.
We come back nevermore.

On the Finding of a UXB on the Old Messerschmitt Field in Augsburg, West Germany

for Ilse Aichinger

1

We lived in the new quarter
above the old airfield
where workers dug and built
from can see to cannot.
The flats and houses rose
I couldn't tell how, by magic,
for you and I were slugging it out
at the table, and I only glimpsed
from time to time a moving crane
that dangled concrete slabs outside
the window, in the constant rain.
You with your thicket of verbs,
I with my grammar's black hooks,
sometimes clinching you to me,
often feeling you slide
under your tongue's thick surface –
no wonder I was thrilled when a bulldozer
nudged the covers off an unexploded bomb
asleep in the old airfield more than 40 years,
not precisely like the Prince who wakened Beauty
with a kiss, but anyway a link to you
that I could understand.

2

That night some gypsies
camped on the edge of the airfield,
the part not excavated. They had big cars –
Mercedes, Cadillacs,
and campers with kitchens.
Why then the little watch-fires?
For after the workmen went home
and the sunset drained in the earth,
the little flares like punctuation
on the red horizon....
I left you alone for a time,
stopped teasing you out like a fuse
from a ticking clock. On the other side
of the window, I waited
for the bomb's *wump*.

3

Which did not come. The UXB
got safely herded back to scrap.
Still, you walked with me
to the cavity, together on the duckboards
over the mud. You didn't like it much,
your country and its spiraling ghost airplanes.
You had nothing to say
about that part of me that wished
the UXB awake and angry and not a stone
left standing on a stone.
A place I loved because of its disasters.

4

Nor were you fond of me
trying to sneak you over the border
of my language. It rained
and it was raining, it did rain
in all the tenses while you said
you loved the children, and not to understand you
too easily, you had not yet begun to forgive yourself
for living your life. I sat alone in a small room
and tried to remember. Outside, the sheep
with their day-glo ID rumps set out to eat
whatever green there was
before the bulldozers came again
to scrape the field.

Against Perfection

I used to feel helpless driving home
and pulling into town – the waves
of his qualified love licking upward,
his slow tug on me, down.
Now I press my finger under the breastbone
to remember that loss radiates
from the circle, and animates my arms and legs.
That keeps me moving, sends out filaments
into the flawed fabric of the one another.
A photograph: a sepia oval of light,
Mother inside it, reading to me,
my sister waiting inside her, listening too.
Ovals and rounds, her face, my arm
around her neck as I lean into the story.
Daddy saw and made this picture; he
was always outside, a tear in the circle,
and that was his appointed part: to show
the necessary rent
in the circle of imperfect human love.

Effigy

The reluctance of a body
to become a thing...and yet
there are those who wish to be stone.

When I think of his face
I think effigy, semblance, counterpart,
tracing, copy, I call up a stone mask

over which a fountain trickles, or a
wooden mask, leafy vines coiling from
mouth and eyes. Both could be my father,

quite natural in this landscape, recognized,
familial and alien at once. Had he been given
the choice between tree and stone, I suppose

he would have chosen to be "tree," even here
in November where the wind probes the gray throats
of steeples, and black barges flatten the river.

The Inner Life

was never what they wanted. They built themselves
an awkward house, too tall, with gawky shrubs
out front, and called it home. It wasn't home,
not "heimat," home and homeland, place
where you are known and you know everything,
but a brick house in the rawest part of town.
While they nailed down the hardwood planks,
the kids played war outside in freshly dug
clay trenches, dangerous, the start of someone's
basement rec room. The parents felt
they had to be pleased but they were not.
The war was not over, promises were due,
but the clumsiness, the stumbling quality
of the house never disappeared, no matter what.
And while the kids camped out by the half-finished
fireplace, while the parents hammered down
another bag of nails and under the radio's arch
the yellow dial blabbed their favorite quiz show,
they laughed at the latest dumb contestant
who couldn't punch his way out of a paper bag.

Grandma Remembered

how wrong it was that her in-laws,
those Old Country ogres from a tale,
sent her out into the cold
driving their pony cart down the frozen hill,
new baby at her breast and a load
of vegetables to sell; how she tried
to nurse my mother there in the open market,
wrapped in her shawls; how some American woman
said Come in, warm yourself, nurse your baby
here by the stove; how Grandma was
desperate enough and wise enough to say yes;
how she saw things in that kitchen
she didn't have names for yet:
cook-stove, curtains,
gingham apron, coffee cup;
how she swallowed her pride to say yes
to compassion, and how she never forgot it.

Widow's Song

No no we'd never
marry again, sing
the widowed sisters.
Having paid so much
the once, we've nothing
left to give again,
not the tiny artifacts
of marriage or the large.
We willed this one thing,
steady, slow, this love
that reached through time
and place, handfasted
only once. They
who chose the food
the side of the bed
the house the car
the work who chose us
for our maidenhead
and benediction
at deathbed
had all of us, we measured
nothing nor held back.
We used up, wore out,
made it do or did without.
Oh no we'd never
marry again, sing
the widowed sisters.

Divorce Witness

Wrong, the ache of this October day,
the passionate burn of leaves, light surgically clear,
and I don't want to be in this courtroom returning
Kathy's rictus of a smile, Chuck's hearty grip.
But they mean to reassure the judge, the lawyers, me.
There'll be no scenes and I am merely a kind of maid,
meant to assist these doings, to answer:
"Do you know this man, this woman?
In your opinion, is this marriage broken?"
The autumn light's a rational probe
that should cut the thickness in my throat.
Shouldn't my words be weighty, ceremonial?
Kathy and Chuck exchange a worried, married look.
Shouldn't there be shouts, recriminations, pleas?
Is this marriage broken?
To everyone's relief, I say, "Irrevocably."

For Mothers

Here comes your daughter Scowl
grown-up at last and waving
her ledger of your many sins
committed and omitted,
a lack of Sunday dinners, or else
too many gray potatoes and more relatives
than anyone needed. In just this
and that you've failed her. You
were always reading or gazing out windows
when she really wanted to talk or else
etcetera etcetera. It's amazing:
your real sins go unnoticed and unnamed:
the days when you welcomed in
the death of love, propped him up
at table, fed him, told him jokes;
how you braided truth and the unspeakable,
or rather, passed on an instinct for evasion;
all those big comfortable lies:
You will never be alone.
There are no last good-byes.

Ghazal: For the Out-of-Work Man

I crossed by foot on the cold mornings, saw
icy tusks hanging from each bronze panther's jaw,

the white disk of pond below the bridge refractive,
self-contained; air like mother-of-pearl and raw

cracked opal, color spread on spires and nets of branches.
I knew he was back in the house chained to a snarl

of wire, acid, oil, deep in the coils of his anger.
Still I wanted for nothing on the bridge, drawn

on by another day, the outlined tasks, and happy
to be there, a piece of the morning, a part

of the landscape, blessed dailiness of walking
past the four poised panthers, mist withdrawn

from offices, joggers, dogs, kids sliding to school.
The habit of joy: my willed amnesia to ignore

the afternoons, the slow walk back, the pause
before fumbling the key at the front door, the inward

suck of heated air, then having to share the small
meal which had simmered all day on the stove.

Love and Work

Six or eight swallows dip to the pond's
green glass, skimming for midges
which rise to meet them: the swallows
double in the calm surface like an eddy of leaves
caught by the wind in a pattern that looks like art
but isn't. Just a beautiful accident
of clear water and the embroidering birds,
but when love and work combine, there is
no difference. I had a friend
whose life moved like these birds, and if ever
he entertained one fake notion about himself, or art,
love or work, I never knew it. As everything floats away,
the swallows' liquid calls upborne over the pond,
I remember his soft chant: So be it, so be it.

Come Home Soon

I was weeding around the tomato plants,
careless and working too fast, it was hot,
I was trying to kill off those choking
morning glory vines we hate but
I caught the hoe in the mint patch instead.
When the mint broke open on the air,
its generous sweet self brought you
back to me, though you're half a world away –
how the mint gave itself, and how its
compassionate heart kept coming back for more.
I love that about even the pesky
morning glory – perennials, as tough as we are.

Juarez, 1978

for Raymond Carver

We were ten years younger, literary,
so when the six bulls, identical, black,
were danced with and formally killed one by one,
it seemed to us that the same bull was killed,
the sand raked clean then bloodied by the same bull;
we took this as a sign that life goes on.
Death was a foreign liturgy, or little more
than a reliquary you could hold in one hand,
exotic as a jeweled toe and finger bone
from a sainted Raimundo or Luz.
I'd still believe this if I could, but I have proof
that death is wildly improvisational, informal,
he doesn't draw between the lines and he never
does the same thing twice. See here,
the failed machinery of my father's heart.
And there, your slow falling, petal by petal.

Odometer

Kids and all, we shored up on El Paso,
rode that prehistoric ocean floor, that backside
of the moon, held on to one another for dear life,
unpacked in the cheap apartment near the Rio Grande's
dusty crooked line. And called you up, Raymond,
because our yellow two-door Chevy's odometer was due
to turn 100,000 miles, and we knew you wouldn't
want to miss that. So around the apartment's
parking lot we drove and drove – it took
longer than we thought, to drive two miles
in a circle – then the odometer turned over
and we cheered and got on with our lives,
mostly frantic in those days, trying to stay on top
of all the payments that had all come due.
We dug out, patched up, pieced it together;
then we had ten good years. And now I've heard
that at the end you couldn't sit still.
That on the last night you circled the room,
pacing from chair to bed; you wouldn't sleep,
tried to stay awake, no one knows how. We think
you were afraid, and that you stayed inside, circling,
trying hard not to move on to where you had to go.

Whenever Someone I Love Gets Sick I Get Angry

which is my way of being afraid. I take
their illnesses to heart, that is, to my unarmed
heart, which seems for a perilous few minutes
to be exposed like the embarrassing Sacred Heart
lithograph of my childhood: a lurid Jesus
who pointed to the heart-shaped heart laid open
in his chest, a looney smile on his movie-
starlet face. But the picture stood for
something true – open your heart, pain will follow.
Last night when our grown child, bent over in pain,
came to our room for help we scrambled from bed
as though we'd nursed her yesterday,
and again I felt my heart thub-lug in anger and in fear.
So many years ago, when I was a child, I too
woke my parents. I was on fire, and my red-faced father
was helpless to soothe me; he drove me screaming to the hospital
while he screamed too, cursing and hitting the steering wheel
in anger and in fear. So when I am angry with your fevers,
when I say "don't die" so fiercely, I want you to hear
"I love you," the full weight of those words.

Notes on Ilse Aichinger and Translations from *Verschenkter Rat*

Ilse Aichinger, born in Vienna in 1921, was one of the first German language writers to attract a large audience in post-war Germany. Today, she is known primarily as a writer of short fiction and radio plays. My translations are selected from her one collection of poems, *Verschenkter Rat* (Advice for Nothing). This collection is not available in English, although her *Selected Poetry and Prose* (translated by Allen H. Chappel and published by Logbridge-Rhodes in 1983) is currently in print.

Aichinger's family was torn apart during the *Anschluss* in 1938. Her Jewish mother, a physician, was forbidden to practice medicine; her Jewish grandmother and other relatives were killed; Aichinger, who had planned to study medicine, was forbidden to do so. When her father deserted the family, she and her mother lived precariously under the protection of her father's non-Jewish relatives; and managed to survive the war. After the war she began medical studies, but soon abandoned them in order to write. She married the German poet Günter Eich in 1953. Following his death in 1972, she, her two children and her mother lived in a small village on the Austrian border. Aichinger currently lives in Frankfurt.

While she has received major literary awards in Germany, including the Bremen Prize for Literature and, in 1988, the Weilheim Prize for Literature, her poems have annoyed and even angered some German critics who object to what they view as "self-indulgent hermeticism." So it intrigues me that her most enthusiastic reception has come from non-writers. Most notably, the Weilheim Prize was awarded to her by a jury of schoolchildren. According to *The German Tribune*, the children said that the reason for their decision was "fascination for the language [she] uses in her work, a language that had its effect on young people, even if the meaning is mysterious."

She certainly had this effect on me as I translated her, particularly because the strangeness of the poems belies what seem to be recognizable surfaces. Her poem openings, in particular, deceive in their simplicity; her syntax seems child-like, and the poems often sound like sentences a child might construct when she's just learning to speak. Aichinger's diction, as well, can trip up the unwary reader. While translating her, I found myself checking simple nouns in scores of dictionaries and having long discussions with German friends about the tonal quality of each word in its particular context. And if her vocabulary is deceptively simple, her use of it is not. Aichinger makes you concentrate on the differences between "hearing" and "listening," "to look" and "to observe." She seems to deliberately disable and disarm the German language, and in this process she makes from it something new. The speakers in her poems grope, ask questions, seek the limits of their worlds, but are often left with nothing except the ability to question.

The more I pored over her poems, the closer she seemed to me as a person; I began to imagine her as a wiser, older woman, an aunt perhaps, who wanted to give me moral and worldly instruction but who had too much tact to presume to offer this advice directly.

My view of her as "wise woman" is especially borne out in many poems which possess fairy tale, fantastic qualities and a tenderness toward children that make the verse luminous. Other poems are dark and threatening; they sometimes warn or teach, and sometimes convey the terrible intensity and dream-like quality of a folktale. Aichinger's poems contain the horror of the Third Reich, but as it might be recalled in wisps of nightmares or overheard whispered conversations. Her work focuses on the possibilities and failures of language in the face of these horrors. The emotional energy of her poetry, its anger or tenderness or even humor, seemingly conducts a life of its own, outside of history.

— *P.B.*